Benjamin Franklin's Humor

Also by Paul M. Zall

Abe Lincoln Laughing

Adams on Adams

Ben Franklin Laughing

Blue and Gray Laughing

Franklin on Franklin

Jefferson on Jefferson

Lincoln on Lincoln

Mark Twain Laughing

Washington on Washington

The Wit and Wisdom of the Founding Fathers

BENJAMIN FRANKLIN'S HUMOR

BY PAUL M. ZALL

THE UNIVERSITY PRESS OF KENTUCKY

Publication of this volume was made possible in part by a grant
from the National Endowment for the Humanities.

Scholarly publisher for the Commonwealth,
serving Bellarmine University, Berea College, Centre College of Kentucky,
Eastern Kentucky University, The Filson Historical Society, Georgetown
College, Kentucky Historical Society, Kentucky State University,
Morehead State University, Murray State University, Northern Kentucky
University, Transylvania University, University of Kentucky, University of
Louisville, and Western Kentucky University.

Editorial and Sales Offices: The University Press of Kentucky
663 South Limestone Street, Lexington, Kentucky 40508-4008
www.kentuckypress.com

09 08 07 06 05 5 4 3 2 1

Frontispiece: Portrait of Benjamin Franklin by Charles Van Loo.
Courtesy of the American Philosophical Society.

Library of Congress Cataloging-in-Publication Data

Zall, Paul M.
Benjamin Franklin's humor / by Paul M. Zall.
p. cm.
Includes bibliographical references and index.
ISBN 0-8131-2371-2 (hardcover : alk. paper)
1. Franklin, Benjamin, 1706-1790—Language. 2. Franklin, Benjamin, 1706-1790—Literary style. 3. Franklin, Benjamin, 1706-1790—Quotations. 4. American wit and humor. 5. Franklin, Benjamin, 1706-1790. 6. Statesmen—United States—Biography. I. Title.
E302.6.F8Z35 2005
973.3'092—dc22 2005018025

This book is printed on acid-free recycled paper meeting
the requirements of the American National Standard
for Permanence in Paper for Printed Library Materials.

Manufactured in the United States of America.

Member of the Association of
American University Presses

For Mo Sloane

and Andy Zall

Contents

Preface

A quarter-century ago, I compiled an edition of anecdotes by and about Ben Franklin aimed at charting the growth of his fame as America's enduring voice of good-humored common sense. The present book focuses on how a quintessentially private person used humor to craft the image of an iconic sociable American. Besides noting that mood affected motive and mode, I have identified Franklin's practical purpose in writing and that his topics were timely, that his models were already familiar to his readers, and that his basic theme was how abusing common sense led to perpetual self-delusion.

Selecting Franklin's humor must be subjective. Like the judge who knows pornography when he sees it, people know humor when they laugh at it. My favorite samples of Franklin's humor are those sketches that use a Socratic irony to distance him from his subject. Because his topics were necessarily ephemeral, I have tried in every case to identify the context. Besides identifying the immediate circumstance, model, and intended readers, I have tried to reprint the texts as those readers saw them. Because those sources are generally inaccessible to modern readers, I have cited recent editions in my source notes. Explanatory notes and comments are incorporated in the indented discussions linking each selection. They derive from the resources of the Huntington Library and the unsparing assistance of librarian David Zeidberg and his staff, Lindsay Obregon, Claire V. Fountain, and Evie Cutting.

INTRODUCTION

A Life in Laughter

They used to say that George Washington was first in war, first in peace, and first in the hearts of his countrymen, and Franklin was first in everything else. But at the nation's bicentennial, the mass-circulating *Reader's Digest* replaced Washington in the hearts of his countrymen with Ben Franklin because Franklin represented what Americans liked best about themselves.[1] If Washington was the father of his countrymen, Franklin was their foxy grandpa, the designated humorist they could always rely on for a sharp saying or merry tale with the "Magical power" to cool the heat and dispel "melancholy fumes."[2]

Franklin could have called himself a doctor, diplomat, electrician, frontier general, insurance man, inventor, legislator, librarian, magistrate, newsman, postmaster, promoter, or publisher, but in his will, he called himself merely "printer." In an age when printers were also writers, he wrote humorous pieces for his brother's newspaper in Boston, later for his own *Pennsylvania Gazette* and *Poor Richard's Almanac,* for newspapers in London and Paris, and for pamphlets for fun or propaganda at home and abroad. In journalism, humor gave him a competitive edge and in propaganda, a shield for both attack and defense.

At fifteen, impersonating a feisty widow, Silence Dogood, Franklin wrote a series of comical essays for his brother James's *New-England Courant.* Her pieces helped in James's continuing competition with other printers. Most impressive was the lively way that Mrs. Dogood monitored Bostonians' manners and morals. Her sharp eye for precise detail and keen ear for dialogue and dialect on the streets of cosmopolitan Boston created dramatic immediacy for the new voice of America laughing.

As a new printer in a Philadelphia already overloaded with almanacs, Franklin needed an almanac to stay in business. He impersonated the faux astrologer Poor Richard Saunders, whose mad antics laughed competitors off the field to make Franklin's almanac Philadelphia's favorite. The lively proverbs on prudence, thrift, and industry collected as "The Way to Wealth," one of America's all-time best sellers, was translated into languages of the western world as diverse as Icelandic and Hebrew.

Leavening the columns of his *Pennsylvania Gazette* with comical comments on the passing scene, Franklin also impersonated a gallery of letter-writing eccentrics like the gossip Celia Shortface or the playboy Anthony Afterwit, whose acerbic complaints would ignite a chain reaction from other correspondents, all likewise impersonated by Franklin himself. In the 1760s and early 1770s, Franklin adopted the same kind of comic monologues in London newspapers to ridicule the British government's American policies, as well as the 1780s in Paris newspapers for such whimsical notions as saving daylight to conserve candles.

In conversation and correspondence, Franklin used humor as cover for the natural shyness he tried to overcome through his celebrated system of behavior modification. The 1770s found him still uneasy among strangers, as young Nabby Adams noticed in Paris: "The Dr. is always silent, unless he has some diverting story to tell."[3] His intimate friend Joseph Priestley concurred: "To strangers he was cold and reserved; but where he was intimate, no man indulged more in pleasantry and good humour."[4]

In private as in public, the essence of his humor was impersonation. As he impersonated fictional letter writers whose eccentricities would be immediately familiar, so he imitated up-to-date literary models—Addison and Steele, and later Jonathan Swift—that had been proven popular. He also parodied the style or burlesqued the form of legal documents, even official newspapers. Some of his jokes were so familiar that Franklin needed only to allude to them for comic effect. Slyly alluding to inflated British propaganda, he mentioned the Irish trooper who claimed to have single-handedly captured five of the enemy by surrounding them.[5]

As he agitated on current issues, Franklin further distanced himself with irony and shielded himself with the dramatic immediacy of another form of impersonation, comic apologues. Franklin's apologues were not merely ornamental. Some, like Aesop's fables, illustrated ethical or moral points, but most applied to everyday social and political issues. He illustrated governmental inefficiency, for example, by telling about two sailors idling on deck when the boatswain approaches: "What are you doing there, Jack?" "Nothing," says Jack. "And pray what are you about, Tom?" "I," says Tom, "am helping him."[6]

Franklin applied some of the best apologues to his own problems. When a friend congratulated him on being named ambassador plenipotentiary to the court of France, Franklin told about the two farmers sent to bring home a harrow from a neighbor on their shoulders. One complained that no two men on earth could carry it. "'Poh!' said the other, who was vain of his strength, 'what do you talk of two men? One may carry it. Help it upon my shoulders and see.' As he proceeded with it, the wag kept exclaiming, 'Zounds, how strong you are! I could not have thought it. Why, you are a Samson! . . . But you will kill yourself! Pray put it down and rest a little, or let me bear a part of the weight.' 'No, no,' said he, being more encouraged by the compliments, than oppressed by the burden; 'you shall see I can carry it quite home.' And so he did."[7]

If Franklin's humor had one overarching theme it was the practice of deception—not only deception of others for fun or profit, but self-deception that could lead to delusion. In "The Way to Wealth," Franklin impersonates Poor Richard impersonating Old Father Abraham, who preaches to a crowd waiting for a bazaar to open. Old Father Abraham preaches on prudence and thrift, taking his texts not from the Bible but from *Poor Richard's Almanac.* The gates open and the crowd dashes in, except for Poor Richard, who, moved by his own words, decides not to buy a new suit after all.

The satire of Poor Richard fooled such sharp critics as Mark Twain and D. H. Lawrence into vilifying Franklin, who in fact loved good wine and fine living, as prototype of American Puritans.

Single mother Polly Baker, prosecuted for having five babies out of wedlock, won acquittal and a husband among the judges on the bench. Franklin's impersonation was so effective that historians portrayed her as an actual victim of Puritan persecution. When Franklin revealed the deception, the leading French historian, Abbé Raynal, reassured him that Franklin's fiction was better than other men's truth.[8] No wonder that Balzac praised Franklin's three greatest inventions as the lightning rod, the republic, and the put-on.[9]

For the last eighteen years of his life, Franklin kept reworking another masterpiece of deception, his autobiography.[10] His revisions over those many years help to put his humorous writing in perspective. Although the narrative breaks off at 1757, on the threshold of his career in diplomacy, its aim and tone were colored by the succeeding thirty years, when as elder statesman he helped engineer the Declaration of Independence, the treaty with France that funded the Revolution, the treaty with Britain that ended it, and the convention of 1787 that produced the Constitution. He would find relief in the irony that helped distance himself from events both past and present.

Franklin's first version of the autobiography in 1771 is a yarn threaded with humor. The garrulous, foxy grandpa chortles over the pratfalls and pitfalls of his callow youth, much on the model of Fielding's *Tom Jones.* At age twenty-one, Franklin almost died from pleurisy. Having suffered through every breath, recovery disappointed him, "regretting in some degree that I must now have all that disagreable work to do over again."[11] His London roommate, James Ralph, found work only as a rural schoolmaster. "Unwilling to have it known that he once was so meanly employ'd, he chang'd his Name, & did me the Honour to assume mine."[12]

This is the wry irony of the autobiography as drafted between 1771 and 1775. During war, peacemaking, and old age, Franklin kept revising and adding to it. At the urging of friends, he changed the story from a portrait of the artist as a young man to an apologue on civic virtue for upwardly mobile young America. He gave even humorous scenes a didactic moral. In one episode, a Senecan orator blamed rum for a nocturnal orgy, saying the great Spirit created rum "for Indians to get drunk with." The authorial voice interrupts the narrative: "Indeed if it be the Design of Providence to extirpate these Savages in order to make room for Cultivators of the Earth, it seems not impossible that Rum may be the appointed Means. It has already annihilated all the Tribes who formerly inhabited the Seacoast."[13]

The revisions show Franklin's characteristically cool control suffering from indignation during a decade of hostilities. To the early draft he added a gratuitous blast at the craven behavior of British troops. During the French and Indian War, he said, "They had plundered and stript the Inhabitants, totally ruining some poor Families by disabling them to planting their Corn or do any thing, besides insulting, abusing & confining the People if they remonstrated."[14]

Deeper bitterness apparently enhanced Franklin's memory of certain events. As the narrative breaks off, Franklin's antagonist is "a proud, angry man," Fernando John Paris, lawyer for the proprietors of Pennsylvania. The narrative says that when Franklin sought redress of Pennsylvania's grievances, Paris rejected his petition as "rude." In fact, Paris could not have rejected the petition. He had died earlier. Franklin's memory must have confused him with the two other proud, angry officials who humiliated him in public, Attorney General Alexander Wedderburne and Secretary of State for the Colonies Lord Hillsborough.

Both publicly humiliated Franklin at the height of his honors. His book on electricity in 1751 had made him more popular than Isaac Newton. While representing the colonies in England for ten years, he had been a leading spokesman against British repression. Queried in Parliament about sending troops to police American riots, he warned, "They will not find a rebellion; they may indeed make one."[15] He even met socially sometimes with Prime Minister Lord North and often with Sir John Pringle, obstetrician to the queen.

Prosecutor Wedderburne demolished Franklin's carefully crafted reputation. Before a packed public hearing at a hall known as the Cockpit, Wedderburne gratuitously damned Franklin's "self-centered importance" and accused him of betraying the public trust by stealing private mail. Franklin impersonated a stoic but seethed from injured pride for years.

The autobiography treated pride as Franklin's basic weakness. In his system of behavior modification, he had tried to control thirteen human weaknesses by routinely exercising opposite virtues. Franklin added a thirteenth virtue, Humility. His lifelong effort was to acquire the real humility practiced by Jesus—and, failing that, at least the appearance of it, as put on by Socrates and which became second nature to

Franklin. He rationalized, "A benevolent Man would . . . allow a few Faults in himself, to keep his Friends in Countenance."[16]

Wedderburne's insults in the Cockpit infuriated but did not humble him. Franklin labored in London another year, confident that his guile in diplomacy could prevent open rebellion. But Secretary Lord Hillsborough made matters worse by rejecting still another of Franklin's petitions as rude, "without having read a Word of it."[17] When politics displaced Hillsborough, Franklin felt triumphant and gloried that even the king "has lately been heard to speak of me with great regard."[18]

But he could not forget the Cockpit even on the glorious Sunday morning when the great William Pitt, Lord Chatham, came to Franklin's house seeking his advice on America. Pitt's noble equipage waited at Franklin's door "while People were coming from Church"—an episode the more pleasurable to Franklin as "it happen'd on the very Day 12 month, that the Ministry had taken so much pains to disgrace me before the Privy Council."[19] Three years later, as he signed the treaty with France that financed the Revolution, he wore the same suit of spotted Manchester velvet that he had worn in the Cockpit.

Commenting on his "Character," Franklin confessed, "Costs me nothing to be civil to inferiors, a good deal to be submissive to superiors."[20] If he had trouble controlling pride, he at least converted anger to propaganda. During the war, he composed a fiery letter to William Strahan, his old fellow printer, now a member of Parliament. "You have begun to burn our Towns, and murder our People. Look upon your Hands! They are stained with the Blood of your Relations! You and I were long Friends; You are now my Enemy, and I am, Yours, B Franklin."[21] He did not send the letter to Strahan but circulated it in newspapers at home and abroad.

He would let real anger overflow in other letters never sent. Infuriated by fellow peace commissioner Arthur Lee's constant carping, he addressed him as paranoid, an extreme "proud and angry man" with a "Sick Mind which is forever Tormenting itself with its Jealousies, Suspicions and Fancies."[22] Bitterness would shadow his celebrated appeal for compromise at the Federal Convention. In his eighties, so weak that John Wilson read the speech aloud, Franklin called compromise the cost of living with human nature controlled by men's "Prejudices, their Passions, their Errors of Opinion, their local Interests, and their selfish Views."[23]

In that speech, Franklin could still draw upon the old-time pleasantry and mirth to cool the heat. He resurrected a well-worn anecdote about Protestant Richard Steele's telling Pope Clement XI that the only difference between their two churches was "The Romish church is infallible, and the Church of England is *never in the wrong.*" He also told a recent saying by the Duchess de la Ferté, who, "in a little dispute with her Sister, said, 'I don't know how it happens, Sister, but I meet with nobody but myself who's always in the right.'"

John Adams envied Franklin's inexhaustible resources: "He had wit at will. He had humor that when he pleased was delicate and delightful. He had a satire that was good natured or caustic, Horace or Juvenal, Swift or Rabelais, at his pleasure. He had talents for irony, allegory and fable, that he could adapt with great skill, to the promotion of moral and political truth. He was master of that infantine simplicity, which the French call naïveté, which never fails to charm, in Phadrus and La Fontaine, from the cradle to the grave."[24] Franklin had to go no further than his earliest Silence Dogood critique of Harvard to find a model for his final satire. Commenting on a speech in Congress favoring the slave trade, he composed a serious allegory, a striking one-to-one correspondence of slavery in 1790 America (black) and 1690 Algiers (white).

Scenes of his last years seemed to replicate the exasperating incidents of the 1770s, except that the role of antagonists then played by proud, angry Britishers—Fernando John Paris, prosecutor Wedderburne, Lord Hillsborough—were now played by proud, angry United States congressmen. Franklin had to remind another generation how Congress had sent him to Canada in winter. "Upwards of 70 years of age, he suffered in his health by the hardships of this journey; lodging in the woods, etc., in so inclement a season; but being recovered, the Congress in the same year ordered him to France."[25]

Among the last things Franklin would write was a petition to Congress seeking compensation for a half-century of selfless public service. Congress refused to grant him western lands such as had been awarded to Arthur Lee. They refused franking privileges. And, with echoes of the Cockpit, in denying reparations, they accused Ben Franklin of kiting his accounts.[26] Live by irony; die by irony. Like Secretary Lord Hillsborough earlier, Congress would not even read his petition.[27]

Considering the trajectory of his sixty years in public service, it would be unreasonable to expect a consistent level in the quality of Franklin's humor. The humor for highly competitive journalism and promotional campaigns followed proven models. Private and public humorous writings of the 1760s and early 1770s sharpened with pressures of his mission to London. Besides serving for propaganda, Franklin's humor during the war decade in Paris secured favor by following the prevailing French fashion for genteel bagatelles. Although some erupted in savage anti-British propaganda, other sketches, as in earliest days, joked about contemporary events. In Franklin's last years, the writings produced under constant pain seldom flashed with the old brilliance.

Franklin said, "There can be no real Humour in an Affectation of Humour."[28] He had valued humor as not an end in itself but a means to gaining a competitive edge, disseminating information, or promoting a program. Writing about timely topics with models and material already popular with a mass reading class, Franklin has left an amusing record of everyday life at the birth of our nation. The best of his humor transcends its immediate purpose and continues to evoke undying laughter at shared human experience.

Franklin's stories and sayings are engraved in our culture—"snug as a bug in the rug" or "Nothing can be said to be certain, except death and taxes." Even if he never said it, he is blamed for the smart saying about hanging together or hanging separately. Other such sayings, less well known but more worthy, now surface on the World Wide Web—"Quacks were the greatest lyars in the world—except their patients."[29]

Understanding the importance of the context in which they were told, Jefferson has left the best record of Franklin actually telling stories. Jefferson tells how while in France they heard that partisan Congressmen had hit an impasse and adjourned. "Speaking with Dr. Franklin on this singular disposition of men to quarrel and divide into parties, he gave his sentiments as usual by way of Apologue. He mentioned the Eddystone lighthouse in the British channel as being built on a rock in the mid-channel, was totally inaccessible in winter, from the boisterous character of that sea, in that season. That therefore, for the two keepers employed to keep up the lights, all provisions for the winter were necessarily carried to them in autumn, as they could never be visited again until the return of the milder season. That on the first practicable day in the spring a boat put off to them with fresh supplies. The boatman met at the door one of the Keepers and accosted him with a, *How goes it friend?*

> *Very well.*
> How is your companion?
> I do not know.
> Don't know? Is not he here?
> I can't tell.
> Have not you seen him today?
> No.
> When did you see him?
> Not since last fall.
> You have killed him?
> *Not I, indeed.*

"They were about to lay hold of him, as having certainly murdered his companion; but he desired them to go upstairs and examine for themselves. They went up, and there found the other keeper. They had quarreled it seems soon after being there, had divided into two parties, assigned the cares below to one, and those above to the other, and had never spoken to or seen one another since."[30]

Benjamin Franklin shaped his own image through his impersonations in "The Way to Wealth," the autobiography, and his familiar letters, but like Jefferson, James Madison also helped by recording such charming though distilled apologues as this: "Previous to the [Constitutional] Convention, and whilst the States were seeking their respective regulations, to enlarge as much as possible their share of the general commerce, the Dr. alluding to their jealousies and competitions remarked that it would be best for all of them to let the trade be free, in which case it would level itself, and leave to each its proper share. These contests he said put him in mind of what had once passed between a littl boy & little girl eating milk & bread out of the same bowl, 'Brother,' cried the little girl, 'eat on your own side, you get more than your share.'"[31]

Then, as now, stories and sayings about him accumulated in which neither face nor facetiae were originally Franklin's. A story about him would eventually be assigned to someone else. One tale tells how, entering an inn one stormy night, Franklin finds all the seats around the fireplace occupied by local gentry. When they hear him ask the landlord to feed his horse oysters, the curious gentry troop outside to see a horse eat oysters, leaving the fire to Franklin. A half-century later, the same tale is told about Abe Lincoln, with the oysters turned into catfish.[32] Lincoln had supplanted Franklin in the folklore of their countrymen.

As a confirmed eclectic himself, Franklin would have expected no less. In August 1788, the eclectic periodical *American Museum* retold Franklin's tale about an eccentric Parisian who would offer to abuse English tourists with a hot poker. Refused, he would ask for at least the cost of heating the poker. The *American Museum* embellished the dialogue with cursing on both sides. Franklin reacted by telling about a tale-bearer who reported a dispute between Queen Anne and the Archbishop of Canterbury that "made both the Queen and the Archbishop swear three or four thumping oaths in every sentence." A skeptic interrupted: "But did the Queen and the Archbishop swear so? . . ." "O no, no," says the speaker, "that is only *my way* of telling the story."[33]

1

Silence Dogood

1722–1723

At thirteen, Franklin plunged into print with a timely ballad about lighthouse keeper George Worthylake drowning with two daughters in the heavy November surf of Boston Harbor. A few months later, he followed with another timely ballad on the capture of the notorious pirate Blackbeard off the Carolina coast. Emboldened, he adopted higher models. Having learned to write by imitating Addison and Steele's popular *Spectator* essays, Franklin aspired to their role as censor of morals and manners. He would correct deviations from community standards by exposing them to ridicule. At sixteen, he transplanted their style to Boston in James Franklin's *New-England Courant.* He left no doubt about his model in his first sketch, using many of the *Spectator's* words. No attribution was necessary, because readers would have known Addision and Steele's style anywhere. Such copying, common in Franklin's time, would be considered legitimate imitation.[1]

Franklin, fearing that James never would have published work by a mere boy otherwise, slipped the first "Silence Dogood" essay through the door under cover of darkness and the pseudonym Silence Dogood, a feisty Boston widow lady. The *Courant* ran fourteen of her essays fortnightly from 2 April through 8 October 1722. Mrs. Dogood's timely remarks on society and fashion sometimes resonate with Benjamin Franklin's incipient talents. But the polished writing suggests help from the coterie of writers, the Couranteers, who lounged around brother James's shop to read London literary periodicals and imitate them in articles for the *Courant* under names like Timothy Turnstone and Zechariah Hearwell.[2] The coterie spent the winter of 1721–1722 mocking Rev. Cotton Mather, who branded them "The Hell-Fire Club" for abusing Boston's clergy. Not surprisingly, then, young Franklin crafted the sprightly widow's name from two of Mather's recent tracts, *Silentarius* and *Essays to Do Good.* Why a widow? One-fourth of Boston's adults were widows.[3]

Even more subtle for modern readers (though not for Franklin's contemporaries) is the allusion to Mather's overwrought scene in the third book of his *Magnalia Christi Americana* (pt. 2, chap. 2, p. 77). Sailing from Newbury to Marblehead with his family, preacher John Avery "was by a Wave sweeping him off, immediately wafted away to Heaven," says Mather. Mrs. Dogood indicts a comparably culpable wave for the death of her father.

As he, poor Man, stood upon the Deck rejoycing at my Birth, a merciless Wave entred the Ship, and in one Moment carry'd him beyond Reprieve. This was the *first Day* which I saw, the *last* that was seen by my Father; and thus was my disconsolate Mother at once made both a *Parent* and a *Widow.* [No. 1][4]

Mrs. Dogood's balance of contrasting terms (*first Day and last, Parent and Widow*) will become a hallmark of Franklin's epigrammatic style, as in, "It is not [General Howe] who had taken Philadelphia, but Philadelphia who had taken him."[5] After telling how she owed her writing skill to a country parson who encouraged her love of books, Mrs. Dogood concludes the first chapter with the same sort of front-loaded shot.

I liv'd a chearful Country Life, spending my leisure Time either in some innocent Diversion with the neighbouring females, or in some shady Retirement, with the best of Company, *Books.*

Thus I past away the Time with a Mixture of Profit and Pleasure, having no Affliction but what was imaginary, and created in my own Fancy; as nothing is more common with us Women, than to be grieving for nothing, when we have nothing else to grieve for. [No. 1]

> Aside from Addison and Steele's carefully crafted style, Mrs. Dogood sounds like Daniel Defoe's spunky, smart, and independent heroines, particularly Moll Flanders, whose popular memoirs appeared in January 1722. In a passage for tonal comparison, Mrs. Flanders offers a capsule account of her first marriage: "Modesty forbids me to reveal the Secrets of the Marriage Bed. . . . My Husband was so Fuddled when he came to Bed, that he could not remember in the Morning, whether he had any Conversation [sex] with me or no. . . . It concerns the Story in hand very little, to enter into the farther particulars . . . [of] the five Years that I liv'd with this Husband; only to observe that I had two Children by him, and that at the end of five Year he died: He had been really a very good Husband to me, and we liv'd very agreeably together."[6] In contrast, Mrs. Dogood's account of her last marriage relies on schoolyard innuendo (*fruitless, topping*) for comic effect.

My Reverend Master who had hitherto remained a Batchelor, (after much Meditation on the Eighteenth verse of the Second Chapter of *Genesis,*) took up a Resolution to marry; and having made several unsuccessful fruitless Attempts on the more topping Sort of our Sex, and being tir'd with making troublesome Journeys and Visits to no Purpose, he began unexpectedly to cast a loving Eye upon Me, whom he had brought up cleverly to his Hand. . . .

We lived happily together in the Heighth of conjugal Love and mutual Endearments, for near Seven Years, in which Time we added Two likely Girls and a Boy to the Family of the Dogoods: But alas! When my Sun was in its meridian Altitude, inexorable unrelenting Death, as if he had envy'd my Happiness and Tranquility, and resolv'd to make me entirely miserable by the Loss of so good an Husband, hastened his Flight to the heavenly World, by a sudden unexpected Departure from this. [No. 2]

To prevent her young son, William, from idleness, her boarder, Clericus, advises sending him to Harvard. This induces her to dream about the Temple of Learning devoted to idleness and dissipation. Her sketch contributed to the ongoing feud between the Couranteers and the local clergy. The competing *Boston Gazette* (28 May 1722) claimed the dream was nonsense ("Whoever heard of taking a Plow into a Temple!"). The critic himself talked nonsense in charging plagiarism from Richard Allestree's didactic *The Gentleman's Calling* (1670). Obviously Franklin's model was the allegorical "Vision of Mirza" (1 September 1711), one of the *Spectator's* most popular papers.[7] Where the "Vision of Mirza" scanned generalized vices and virtues, Mrs. Dogood's vision had a local habitation and a name.

I reflected in my Mind on the extream Folly of those Parents who, blind to their Childrens Dulness, and insensible of the Solidity of their Skulls, because they think their Purses can afford it, will needs send them to the Temple of Learning, where, for want of a suitable Genius, they learn little more than how to carry themselves handsomely, and enter a Room genteely, (which might as well be acquir'd at a Dancing-School,) and from whence they return, after Abundance of Trouble and Charge, as great Blockheads as ever, only more proud and self-conceited.

While I was in the midst of these unpleasant Reflections, Clericus (who with a Book in his Hand was walking under the Trees) accidentally awak'd me; to him I related my Dream with all its Particulars, and he, without much Study, presently interpreted it, assuring me, *That it was a lively Representation of HARVARD COLLEGE, Etcetera.* [No. 4]

For her contribution to the Couranteers' ongoing critique of women's society and fashion, Mrs. Dogood had—besides the *Spectator*—many models in the London popular press as, for example, in the weekly *British Apollo,* Defoe's *Review,* or London's *Penny-Post.* But her model lay closer to home in the frequent columns by Couranteer Nathaniel Gardner. Franklin adopted his device of chatting with correspondents (himself under assumed names). For example, Mrs. Dogood responds to criticism from "Ephraim Censorious" by publishing his letter. The trick here is to distinguish her style from that of her correspondent, which Franklin reinforces by concluding "Ephraim's" letter with salacious innuendo.

Let the first Volley of your Resentments be directed against *Female* Vice; let Female Idleness, Ignorance and Folly, (which are Vices more peculiar to your Sex than to our's,) be the Subject of your Satyrs, but more especially Female Pride, which I think is intollerable. Here is a large Field that wants Cultivation, and which I believe you are able (if willing) to improve with Advantage; and when you have once reformed the Women, you will find it a much easier Task to reform the Men, because Women are the prime Causes of a great many Male Enormities. [No. 5]

With an eye to print-shop business, Mrs. Dogood's satire on the vanity of "Hoop-Petticoats" offers comical treatment of a quasi-religious pamphlet published in the same year by James Franklin. The anonymous author of *Hoop-Petticoats Arraigned and Condemned by the Light of Nature and Law of God* sends a simple message to women of fashion: "Methinks they would do well to consider, that *strait is the gate,* & narrow the way that leads to Life; and whether their extensive Hoops may not be some hindrance unto them in walking this narrow way" (3). Mrs. Dogood also yokes incongruous images in a solution both comical and sensible, prefiguring the Paris citizen who later proposes daylight savings. She had another model in the *Spectator* (26 July 1711), which also exaggerated the image of hoopskirts as fortification ("Outworks and Lines of Circumvallation"). In keeping a more exaggerated caricature under control, Franklin at age sixteen displayed a major advance in keeping comic imagery credible.

These monstrous topsy-turvy *Mortar-Pieces,* are neither fit for the Church, the Hall, or the Kitchen; and if a Number of them were well mounted on *Noddles-Island,* they would look more like Engines of War for bombarding the Town, than Ornaments of the Fair Sex. An honest Neighbour of mine, happening to be in Town some time since on a publick Day, inform'd me, that he saw four Gentlewomen with their Hoops half mounted in a Balcony, as they withdrew to the Wall, to the great terror of the Militia, who (he thinks) might attribute their irregular Volleys to the formidable Appearance of the Ladies Petticoats.

I assure you, Sir, I have but little Hopes of perswading my Sex, by this Letter, utterly to relinquish the extravagant Foolery, and Indication of Immodesty, in this monstrous Garb of their's; but I would at least desire them to lessen the Circumference of their Hoops, and leave it with them to consider, Whether they, who pay no Rates or Taxes, ought to take up more Room in the King's High-Way, than the Men, who yearly contribute to the Support of the Government. [No. 6]

Another exercise in comic technique of a different sort foreshadows Franklin's deadpan style in mocking the gullibility of competing almanac maker, Titan Leeds, and also previews the theme of the classic "Old Mistresses Apologue." The present sketch follows directly from Mrs. Dogood's tenth essay, which chiefly reprinted extracts from Defoe's *Essay on Projects* proposing an insurance plan for indigent widows. It differs from a petition by "Chastity Loveworth" in the *Spectator* (9 February 1712) against women who spoil suitors for other women: the petition from Mrs. Dogood's correspondent guilelessly reveals a more selfish motive.

1. That your Petitioner being puff'd up in her younger Years with a numerous Train of Humble Servants, had the Vanity to think, that her extraordinary Wit and Beauty would continually recommend her to the Esteem of the Gallants; and therefore as soon as it came to be publickly known that any gentleman address'd her, he was immediately discarded.

2. That several of your Petitioners Humble Servants, who upon their being rejected by her, were, to all Apperance in a dying Condition, have since recover'd their Health, and been several Years married, to the great Surprize and Grief of your Petitioner, who parted with them upon no other Conditions, but that they should die or run distracted for her, as several of them faithfully promis'd to do.

3. That your Petititoner finding her self disappointed in and neglected by her former Adorers, and no new Offers appearing for some Years past, she has been industriously contracting Acquaintance with several Families in Town and Country, where any young Gentlemen or Widowers have resided, and endeavour'd to appear as conversable as possible before them: She has likewise been a strict Observer of the Fashion, and always appear'd well dress'd. And the better to restore her decay'd Beauty, she has consum'd above Fifty Pound's Worth of the most approved *Cosmeticks.* But all won't do.

Your Petitioner therefore most humbly prays, That you would be pleased to form a Project for the Relief of all those penitent Mortals of the fair Sex, that are like to be punish'd with their Virginity until old Age, for the Pride and Insolence of their Youth.

And your Petitioner (as in Duty bound) shall ever pray, &c.

Margaret Aftercast.

Were I endow'd with the Faculty of Matchmaking, it should be improv'd for the Benefit of Mrs. Margaret, and others in her Condition: But since my extream Modesty and Taciturnity, forbids an Attempt of this Nature, I would advise them to relieve themselves in a Method of Friendly Society . . . whereby every single Woman, upon full Proof given of her continuing a Virgin for the Space of Eighteen Years, (dating her Virginity from the Age of Twelve,) should be entituled to 500 Pounds in ready Cash. [No. 11]

A few years earlier, Franklin's initial plunge into print had been sailors' ballads on timely topics, such as the capture of Blackbeard and the drowning of the local lighthouse keeper. Now, to show that every doggerel hath its day, Mrs. Dogood comments on a poem by Dr. John Herrick.[8] She is up to date in supporting Isaac Watts's efforts to restore common sense and common language to poetry—"plain Narration and a simple Dress,"[9] modeled on the words, if not the music, of Alexander Pope's popular "Receit to make an Epick Poem."[10] Franklin burlesques the form, parodies the content of a specific poem, and creates a new category for Kitelic verse. If nothing else, the sustained, cool control of Mrs. Dogood's exaggerated encomium hints at corporate authorship among the Couranteers lounging in James Franklin's shop.

It has been the Complaint of many Ingenious Foreigners, who have travell'd amongst us, *That good Poetry is not to be expected in* New-England. I am apt to Fancy, the Reason is, not because our Countreymen are altogether void of a Poetical Genius, nor yet because we have not those Advantages of Education which other Countries have, but purely because we do not afford that Praise and Encouragement which is merited, when any thing extraordinary of this Kind is produc'd among us: Upon which Consideration I have determined, when I meet with a Good Piece of *New-England* Poetry, to give it a suitable Encomium, and thereby endeavour to discover to the World some of its Beautys, in order to encourage the Author to go on, and bless the World with more, and more Excellent Productions.

There has lately appear'd among us a most Excellent Piece of Poetry, entituled, *An Elegy upon the much Lamented Death of Mrs. Mehitebell Kitel, Wife of Mr. John Kitel of Salem, &c.* It may justly be said in its Praise, without Flattery to the Author, that it is the most *Extraordinary* Piece that ever was wrote in *New-England*. The Language is so soft and Easy, the Expression so moving and pathetick, but above all, the Verse and Numbers so Charming and Natural, that it is almost beyond Comparison,

The Muse disdains
Those Links and Chains,

Measures and Rules of vulgar Strains,
And o'er the Laws of Harmony a Sovereign Queen she reigns.
—Watts ["Two Happy Rivals," 11–14, *Horae Lyricae* (1709)]

I find no English Author, Ancient or Modern, whose Elegies may be compar'd with this, in respect to the Elegance of Stile, or Smoothness of Rhime; and for the affecting Part, I will leave your Readers to judge, if ever they read any Lines, that would sooner make them *draw their Breath* and Sigh, if not shed Tears, than these following.

Come let us mourn, for we have lost a Wife, a Daughter, and a Sister
Who has lately taken Flight, and greatly we have mist her.

In another Place,

Some little Time before she yielded up her Breath,
She said, I ne'er shall hear one Sermon more on Earth
She kist her Husband some little Time before she expir'd,
Then lean'd her Head the Pillow on, just out of Breath and tir'd.

BUT the Threefold Appellation in the first Line

—a Wife, a Daughter, and a Sister,

must not pass unobserved. That Line in the celebrated Watts,

Gunston the Just, the Generous, and the Young,

is nothing Comparable to it. The latter only mentions three Qualifications of *one* Person who was deceased, which therefore could raise Grief and Compassion but for *One*. Whereas the former, (*our most excellent Poet*) gives his Reader a Sort of an Idea of the Death of *Three Persons,* viz.

—a Wife, a Daughter, and a Sister,

which is *Three Times* as great a Loss as the Death of *One,* and consequently must raise *Three Times* as much Grief and Compassion in the Reader.

I should be very much straitned for Room, if I should attempt to discover even half the Excellencies of this Elegy which are obvious to me. Yet I cannot omit one Observation, which is, that the Author has (to his Honour) invented a new Species of Poetry, which wants a Name, and was never before known. His Muse scorns to be confin'd to the old Measures and Limits, or to observe the dull Rules of Criticks. . . .

Now 'tis Pity that such an Excellent Piece should not be dignify'd with a particular Name; and seeing it cannot justly be called, either *Epic, Sapphic, Lyric,* or *Pindaric,* nor any other Name yet invented, I presume it may, (in Honour and Remembrance of the Dead) be called the KITELIC. Thus much in the Praise of *Kitelic Poetry.*

It is certain, that those Elegies which are of our own Growth, (and our Soil seldom produces any other sort of Poetry) are by far the greatest part, wretchedly Dull and Ridiculous. Now since it is imagin'd by many, that our Poets are honest, well-meaning Fellows, who do their best, and that if they had but some Instructions how to govern Fancy with Judgment, they would make indifferent good Elegies, I shall here subjoin a Receipt for that purpose, which was left me as a Legacy, (among other valuable Rarities) by my Reverend Husband. It is as follows,

A RECEIPT to make a New-England
Funeral ELEGY

For the Title of your Elegy. *Of these you may have enough ready made to your Hands; but if you should chuse to make it your self, you must be sure not to omit the Words* Aetatis Suae [at age of], *which will Beautify it exceedingly.*

For the Subject of your Elegy. *Take one of your Neighbours who has lately departed this Life; it is no great matter at which Age the Party dy'd, but it will be best if he went away suddenly, being Kill'd, Drown'd, or Froze to Death.*

Having chose the Person, take all his Virtues, Excellencies, &c. and if he have not enough, you may borrow some to make up a sufficient Quantity: To these add his Last Words, dying Expressions, &c. if they are to be had; mix all these together, and be sure you strain *them well. Then season all with a Handful or two of Melancholly Expressions, such as,* Dreadful, Deadly, cruel cold Death, unhappy Fate, weeping eyes, &c. *Have mixed all these Ingredients well, put them into the empty Scull of some* young Harvard; (*but in Case you have ne'er a One at Hand, you may use your own,) there let them Ferment for the Space of a Fortnight, and by that Time they will be incorporated into a Body, which take out, and having prepared a sufficient Quantity of double Rhimes, such as* Power, Flower; Quiver, Shiver; Grieve us, Leave us; tell you, excel you; Expeditions, Physicians; Fatigue him, Intrigue him, &c. *you must spread all upon Paper, and if you can procure a Scrap of Latin to put at the End, it will garnish it mightily; then having affixed your Name at the Bottom, with a Moestus Composuit* [writ in sorrow], *you will have an Excellent Elegy.*

N.B. *This receipt will serve when a Female is the Subject of your elegy, provided you borrow a greater Quantity of Virtues, Excellencies, &c.* [No. 7]

In 1722, Mrs. Dogood must have known that Boston's wine was safer than the water. With a population near 10,000, there was one liquor retailer for about every twenty families.[11] As censor of public morals, Mrs. Dogood deplored excessive drinking as uncontrolled self-indulgence and self-deception. Franklin could easily have been parodying such temperance sermons as Benjamin Wadsworth's *An Essay to Do Good* (Boston, 1710) whose description of "gross common Drunkards" includes descriptions like, "Staggering, Yawning, Slavering, Wallowing in His Vomit; or so Stupefy'd that he can't move any more than a log" (A4). More timely would be acknowledging a new dictionary to compete with Thomas Blount's old-fashioned favorite, *Glossographia.* Nathaniel Bailey had just published *An Universal Etymological English Dictionary* featuring such pertinent terms as "Bowse—to drink stoutly," and the term "mellow" to describe being drunk. Mrs. Dogood's own list derives from Franklin's experience as well as authority, and with age, it expanded from 19 terms to 228 in the *Pennsylvania Gazette* (6 January 1738).[12]

The wordplay covers more serious purpose. Franklin here and hereafter, in private and public, exaggerates how reasonable men will find or make a reason for anything they have a mind to do. Again, very sophisticated for a sixteen-year-old, he treats drinking to excess as appetite acquired by habit, a social folly affecting character as well as manners.

As the Effects of Liquor are various, so are the Characters given to its Devourers. It argues some Shame in the Drunkards themselves, in that they have invented numberless Words and Phrases to cover their Folly, whose proper Significations are harmless, or have no Signification at all. They are seldom known to be "drunk," tho they are very often "boozey, cogey, tipsey, fox'd, merry, mellow, fuddl'd, groatable, Confoundedly cut, See two Moons, are Among the Philistines, In a very good Humour, See the Sun, or, The Sun has shone upon them; they Clip the King's English, are Almost froze, Feavourish, In their Attitudes, Pretty well enter'd, &c." In short, every Day produces some new Word or Phrase which might be added to the Vocabulary of the "Tiplers": But I have chose to mention these few, because if at any Time a Man of Sobriety and Temperance happens to "cut himself confoundedly," or is "almost froze," or "fevourish," or accidentally "sees the Sun," &c. he may escape the Imputation of being "drunk," when his Misfortune comes to be related. [No. 12]

Allying temperance with chastity, Mrs. Dogood tells about a night ramble that revealed sex in the city openly enjoyed on the streets.

Her lively description follows a series of pieces (by Couranteer Captain Christopher Taylor) in the *Courant* (26 February, 2 April, 9 April) on rampant illicit sex. Her model, however, was Nathaniel Gardner's anonymous sketch of his own reception by women of the street after the *Courant* had accused them of idleness and vanity: "It was with no small Pleasure that I heard my self rail'd at the other Night by a couple of Females, as I pass'd along the Street. After their Gallant had inform'd them who I was, they broke out, *Well! That's he that we saw t'other Day to be sure. I desire to be satisfy'd! He's the ugliest Fellow that I ever saw in my Life.—He's short Neck'd, stubbed Shank'd, rusty Hair'd,—Lawful Heart! He's deform'd, and dull, and every thing.* [26 February 1722].

In one of the late pleasant Moon-light Evenings, I so far indulg'd in my self the Humour of the Town in walking abroad, as to continue from my Lodgings two or three Hours later than usual, & was pleas'd beyond Expectation before my Return. Here I found various Company to observe, and various Discourse to attend to. I met indeed with the common fate of *Listeners, (who hear no good of themselves,)* but from a Consciousness of my Innocence, receiv'd it with a Satisfaction beyond what the Love of Flattery and the Daubings of a Parasite could produce.

The Company who rally'd me were about Twenty in Number, of both Sexes; and tho' the *Confusion of Tongues* (like that of *Babel*) which always happens among so many impetuous Talkers, render'd their Discourse not so intelligible as I could wish, I learnt thus much, That one of the Females pretended to know me, from some Discourse she had heard at a certain House before the Publication of one of my Letters; adding, *That I was a Person of an ill Character, and kept a criminal Correspondence with a Gentleman who assisted me in Writing.* One of the Gallants clear'd me of this random Charge, by saying, *That tho' I wrote in the Character of a Woman, he knew me to be a Man; But,* continu'd he, *he has more need of endeavouring a Reformation in himself, than spending his Wit in satyrizing others.*

I had no sooner left this Set of Ramblers, but I met a Crowd of

Tarpolins and their Doxies, link'd to each other by the Arms, who ran (by their own Account) after the Rate of *Six Knots an Hour,* and bent their Course towards the *Common.* Their eager and amorous Emotions of Body, occasion'd by taking their Mistresses *in Tow,* they call'd *wild Steerage:* And as a Pair of them happen'd to trip and come to the Ground, the Company were call'd upon to *bring to,* for that *Jack* and *Betty* were *founder'd.*

But this Fleet were not less comical or irregular in their Progress than a Company of Females I soon after came up with, who, by throwing their Heads to the Right and Left, at every one who pass'd by them, I concluded came out with no other Design than to revive the Spirit of Love in Disappointed Batchelors, and expose themselves to Sale to the first Bidder.

But it would take up too much Room . . . to mention all the Occasions of Diversion I met with in this Night's Ramble. As it grew later, I observed, that many pensive Youths with down Looks and a slow Pace, would be ever now and then crying out on the Cruelty of their Mistresses; others with a more rapid Pace and chearful Air, would be swinging their Canes, and clapping their Cheeks, and whispering at certain Intervals, *I'm certain I shall have her! This is more than I expected! How charmingly she talks! &c.*

Upon the whole I conclude, That our *Night-Walkers* are a set of People, who contribute very much to the Health and Satisfaction of those who have been fatigu'd with Business or Study, and occasionally observe their pretty Gestures and Impertinencies. But among Men of Business, the *Shoemakers,* and other Dealers in Leather, are doubly oblig'd to them, inasmuch as they exceedingly promote the Consumption of their Ware: And I have heard of a *Shoemaker,* who being ask'd by a noted Rambler, *Whether he could tell how long her Shoes would last;* very prettily answer'd, *That he knew how many Days she might wear them, but not how many Nights, because they were then put to a more violent and irregular Service, than when she employ'd her self in the common Affairs of the House.* [No. 13]

Mrs. Dogood's fourteenth and final letter simply abstracted passages from a series about church and state in the *London*

Journal, "Cato's Letters" (4 February 1720/1). Her sketch about night walking represented the height of a learning curve that began with Franklin imitating the narrative method of Addison and Steele. After a mere seven months, he could imitate the more dramatic methods of John Bunyan and Daniel Defoe, whom he praised for mixing "Narration & Dialogue, a Method of Writing very engaging to the Reader, who in the most interesting Parts finds himself as it were brought into the Company, & present at the Discourse."[13] He had learned to dramatize humorous subjects in such a way as to let their words alone reveal their characters. In this respect Franklin had surpassed the Couranteers like Nathaniel Gardner, who had mentored, if not collaborated on, the series.[14]

Franklin's circumstances ceased to be amusing. During 1722–1723, local authorities, indignant at the *Courant's* constant sniping, twice jailed James Franklin. Benjamin Franklin, who was listed as editor of the *New-England Courant* after his brother was jailed, risked jail himself, especially after Mrs. Dogood's ninth sketch attacked clergy who manipulated politicians. Franklin would later claim his brother's abuse drove him to break his apprentice bond and leave town. More romantically, his excuse was that he had gotten a girl pregnant. Whatever the case, in September 1723, at the age of seventeen, he sallied forth to face life friendless in Philadelphia.

2

Paragraphs in Philadelphia

1729–1735

Except for two impoverished years at London, youthful Franklin flourished in Philadelphia. He printed with Samuel Keimer until 1728 when he broke off to start his own shop. Keimer then published *The Universal Instructor . . . or Pennsylvania Gazette.* He claimed that the city's only newspaper, Andrew Bradford's *American Weekly Mercury,* was too frivolous, but that excuse hid the fact that Keimer was undercutting Franklin's plan to start his own newspaper. Keimer reached peak circulation of about 250[1] but lost readers as Franklin, for vengeance, mocked him in the *Mercury.* When Keimer merely reprinted an encyclopedic piece on abortion, complete with defintions, symptoms, and prescriptions, Franklin as Martha Careful and Caelia Shortface ridiculed the article as too licentious for virtuous women readers. The two brief letters in the *Mercury* for 28 January 1729 were remarkable otherwise only for displaying Franklin's ability to differentiate individual comic voices, as in these samples:

Martha Careful—My Sister Molly and my Self, with some others, are Resolved to run the Hazard of taking him by the Beard, at the next Place we meet him, and make an Example of him for his Immodesty.

Caelia Shortface (with Quaker "thee," "thou," and "thy")—I was last Night in Company with several of my Acquaintance, and Thee, and *Thy Indecencies,* was the Subject of our Discourse, but at last we Resolved, That if thou Continue . . . to make Thy Ears suffer for it.

For the next two months (4 February to 27 March 1729), he composed a half-dozen essays. As the "Busy-Body," Franklin continued to follow the methods, but no longer slavishly imitated the style, of the *Spectator.*[2] He sketched typical samples of vice and virtue by using stylized "characters" but with ironic twists of such names as Ridentius. His second sketch played variations on the theme of *Spectator* No. 249 as Ridentius mocks other persons with sneers "that shall pass for Wit, Noise for Reason, and the Strength of Argument . . . judg'd by that of the Lungs." Despite the lively details, compared to his best Silence Dogood sketches, Franklin's second Busy-Body sketch uses invective and direct narration rather than understated, dramatic scenes—and accordingly achieves weaker humorous effect.

Let us take a view of Ridentius: What a contemptible Figure does he make with his Train of paultry Admirers? This Wight shall give himself an Hours Diversion with the Cock of a Man's Hat, the Heels of his Shoes, an unguarded Expression in his Discourse, or even some Personal Defect; and the Height of his low Ambition is to put some One of the Company to the Blush, who perhaps must pay an equal Share of the Reckoning with himself. If such a Fellow makes Laughing the sole End and Purpose of his Life, if it is necessary to his Constitution, or if he has a great Desire of growing suddenly fat, let him treat; let him give publick Notice where any dull stupid Rogues may get a Quart of Fourpenny [ale] for being laugh'd at; but 'tis barbarously unhandsome, when Friends meet for the Benefit of Conversation, and a proper Relaxation from Business, that one should be the *Butt* of the Company, and Four Men made merry at the Cost of the Fifth. [No. 2][3]

Franklin's next Busy-Body sketch plays on the theme of *Spectator* No. 243, which contrasts men of probity and virtue with those who blacken and defame them. Busy-Body contrasts the virtues of a rustic gentleman of fortune, Cato, with the vices of a well-known villain, here called Cretico, whom he dissects with sharp invective.

O Cretico! Thou sowre Philosopher! Thou cunning Statesman! Thou art crafty, but far from being Wise. When wilt thou be esteem'd, regarded and belov'd like *Cato?* When wilt thou, among thy Creatures meet with that unfeign'd Respect and warm Good-will that all Men have for him? Wilt thou never understand that the cringing, mean, submissive Deportment of thy dependants, is (like the Worship paid by *Indians* to the Devil) rather thro' Fear of the Harm thou may'st do to them, than out of Gratitude for the Favours they have receiv'd of thee?. . . [Busy-Body appends an ambiguous disclaimer.] *'Tis to be observ'd that if any bad Characters happen to be drawn in the Course of these Papers, they mean no particular Person, if they are not particularly apply'd.* [No. 3]

Unlike the Silence Dogood sketches, which treated public problems, Franklin used Busy-Body sketches for a personal vendetta against Samuel Keimer. Keimer, who recognized himself as the original of the "sowre Philosopher," printed a stream of invective against Franklin as "Bebegio," whose merits were "as threadbare as his Great Coat, and Scull as thick as his Shoe-Soles."[4] In the fifth Busy-Body essay, Franklin repelled Keimer's complaints: "*Ill Nature* appears, in his endeavouring to discover Satyr, where I intended no such Thing."[5] Keimer persisted in complaining until September when, bankrupt, he sold the *Pennsylvania Gazette* to Franklin and Hugh Meredith, a partner whose father promised the purchase price.

Meanwhile, Franklin had not entirely abandoned the more amusing style of the Silence Dogood monologues or the model of the *Spectator.* For the fourth Busy-Body piece, he followed *Spectator* No. 155 in talking about problems faced by women shopkeepers. He surpassed his model in comic effect by letting the character subtly reveal herself, in contrast to this direct style of the *Spectator:* "Here is one who makes me once or twice a Week tumble over all my Goods, and then owns it was only a Gallantry to see me act with these pretty Hands; then lays out three Pence in a little Ribband for his Wristbands, and thinks he is a Man of great Vivacity."[6]

Franklin shows the influence of plays he saw during his 1724–1726 stay in London. Harassed "Patience," while complaining about a customer's unruly children, slips into revealing her feelings about being childless. She appeals to the Busy-Body in his self-proclaimed capacity as a "Kind of Censor Morum."

You having set your self up for a *Censuror Morum* (as I think you call it) which is said to mean a *Reformer of Manners,* I know no Person more proper to be apply'd to for Redress in all the Grievances we suffer from *Want of Manners* in some People. You must know I am a single Woman, and keep a Shop in this Town for a Livelyhood. There is a certain Neighbour of mine, who is really agreeable Companion enough, and with whom I have had an Intimacy of some Time standing; But of late she makes her Visits so excessively often, and stays so very long every Visit, that I am tir'd out of all Patience. I have no Manner of Time at all to my self; and you, who seem to be a wise Man, must needs be sensible that every Person has little Secrets and Privacies that are not proper to be expos'd even to the nearest Friend. Now I cannot do the least Thing in the World, but she must know all about it; and it is a Wonder I have found an Opportunity to write you this Letter. . . . But, alas, Sir, I have not yet told you half my Afflictions. She has two children that are just big enough to run about and do pretty Mischief: These are continually along with *Mamma,* either in my Room or Shop, if I have never so many Customers or People with me about Business. Sometimes they pull the Goods off my low Shelves down to the ground, and perhaps where one of them has just been making Water; My Friend takes up the Stuff, and cries, *Eh! thou little wicked mischievous Rogue!—But however, it has done no great Damage; 'tis only wet a little;* and so puts it up upon the Shelf again. Sometimes they get to my Cask of Nails behind the Counter, and divert themselves, to my great Vexation, with mixing my Ten-penny and Eight-penny and Four-penny together. I Endeavour to conceal my Uneasiness as much as possible, and with a grave Look go to Sorting them out. She cries, *Don't thee trouble thy self, Neighbour: Let them play a little; I'll put all to rights my self before I go.* But Things are never so put to rights but that I find a great deal of Work to do after they are gone. Thus, Sir, I have all the Trouble and Pesterment of Children, without the Pleasure of——calling them my own; and they are now so us'd to being here that they will be content no where else. . . . This very Morning they have so tormented me that I could bear no longer; For while the Mother was asking me twenty impertinent Questions, the youngest got to my Nails, and with great Delight rattled them by handfuls all over the Floor; and the other at the same Time made such a terrible Din upon my Counter with a Hammer, that I grew half distracted. I was just then about to make my self a new Suit of Pinners [pinafore], but in the Fret and Confusion I cut it quite out of all Manner of Shape, and utterly spoil'd a Piece of the first Muslin. . . . But I have twenty Things more to tell you besides all this; There is a handsome Gentleman that has a Mind (I don't question) to make love to me, but he can't get the least Opportunity to——O dear, here she comes again—I must conclude. [No. 4]

Franklin flourished in the printing trade thanks to hard work made visible—as in pushing a loaded wheelbarrow through the streets—taking loans from friends, and receiving help from his self-improvement support group, called the "Junto." He would write Junto exercises to be read at meetings, then revise them for his newspaper. He wrote serious papers on civic affairs along with such fashionable humor as his celebrated epitaph that circulated in manuscript from about 1728. As Silence Dogood's night-rambling sailors punned on nautical terms, so the epitaph puns on printers' jargon. Among Franklin's possible models was the serious epitaph for Boston printer John Foster that hoped for resurrection of "a fair Edition & of matchless worth, / Free from Errata."[7] But Franklin's epithet develops a cohesive conceit worthy of the celebrated baroque poet Luis de Góngora.

The Body of
B. Franklin,
Printer;
Like the Cover of an old Book,
Its Contents torn out,
And stript of its Lettering and Gilding,
Lies here, Food for Worms.
But the Work shall not be wholly lost:
For it will, as he believ'd, appear once more,
In a new & more Perfect Edition,
Corrected and amended
By the Author.
He was born Jan. 6. 1706.
Died 17[8]

Franklin's editorial style in the *Pennsylvania Gazette* showed similar control. He spoke directly to the reader in the colloquial, everyday language of conversation. In an age of reading aloud, Franklin's text would provide a script, comical and otherwise, that any reader could perform, as in these paragraph fillers.

—Sometime last Week, we are informed, that one Piles a Fidler, with his Wife, were overset in a Canoo near Newtown Creek. The good Man, 'tis said, prudently secur'd his Fiddle, and let his Wife go to the Bottom. [16 October 1729]

—An unhappy Man one *Sturgis,* upon some Difference with his Wife, determined to drown himself in the River; and she, (kind Wife) went with him, it seems, to see it faithfully performed, and accordingly stood by silent and unconcerned during the whole

Transaction: He jump'd in near *Carpenter's* Wharff, but was timely taken out again, before what he came about was thoroughly effected, so that they were both obliged to return home as they came, and put up for that Time with the Disappointment. [10 February 1730]

—Friday Night last, a certain Stonecutter was, it seems, in a fair way of dying the Death of a Nobleman; for being caught Napping with another Man's Wife, the injur'd Husband took the Advantage of his being fast asleep, and with a Knife began very diligently to cut off his Head. But the Instrument not being equal to the intended Operation, much Struggling prevented Success; and he was oblig'd to content himself for the present with bestowing on the Aggressor a sound Drubbing. The Gap made in the Side of the Stonecutter's Neck, tho' deep, is not thought dangerous; but some People admire, that when the Person offended had so fair and subtle an Opportunity, it did not enter into his Head to turn Stonecutter ["stones" also meant "testicles"] himself. [17 June 1731]

—From New-York, we hear, that on Saturday se'nnight, in the Afternoon, they had there most terrible Thunder and Lightning, but no great Damage done. The same Day we had some very hard Claps in these Parts; and 'tis said, that in Bucks County, one Flash came so near a Lad, as, without hurting him, to melt the Pewter Button off the Wasteband of his Breeches. 'Tis well nothing else thereabouts, was made of Pewter. [15 June 1732]

Franklin did not abandon the mocking strategy used against competitor Keimer, but he used a lighter touch against the competing *Mercury*. Owner Andrew Bradford was, after all, the postmaster who controlled newspaper circulation. Also noticeable was a subtle shift in models from the *Spectator* to the contemporary works of Jonathan Swift. To compete in the printing trade, Franklin used a comical offense as the best defense. As in his conversation, he found self-deprecating humor effective in disarming critics. For example, in excusing a typographical error, he has "J.T." play the role of friendly correspondent, complete with Latin motto, *Printerum est errare,* open to loose interpretation as "To print is to err," or "Every day is the dawn of a new error."

As your last Paper was reading in some Company where I was present, these Words were taken Notice of in the Article concerning Governor Belcher [of Massachusetts] ("His Excellency, with the gentlemen trading to New-England, *died* elegantly at Pontack's"). The Word *died* should doubtless have been *dined* . . . but this Omission of the letter "n" in that Word, gave us as much Entertainment as any Part of your Paper. One took the Opportunity of telling us, that in a certain Edition of the Bible, the Printer had, where David says *I am fearfully and wonderfully made,* omitted the Letter *e* in the last Word, so that it was, *I am fearfully and wonderfully mad;* which occasion'd an ignorant Preacher, who took that Text, to harangue his Audience for half an hour on the Subject of *Spiritual Madness.*

Another related to us, that when the Company of Stationers in England had the Printing of the Bible in their Hands, the Word *not* was left out in the Seventh Commandment, and the whole Edition was printed off with *Thou shalt commit Adultery,* instead of *Thou shalt not, &c.* This material Erratum induc'd the Crown to take the Patent from them which is now held by the King's Printer. The *Spectator*'s Remark upon this Story is, that he doubts many of our modern Gentlemen have this faulty Edition by 'em, and are not made sensible of the Mistake.

Although he modeled that story on the *Spectator* No. 579, Franklin's vernacular style vastly improved the original's bookish comment: "I am afraid that very many young Profligates, of both sexes, are possessed of this spurious Edition of the Bible, and observe the Commandment according to the faulty Reading."[9]

A third Person in the Company acquainted us with an unlucky Fault that went through a whole Impression of Common-

Prayer-Books; in the Funeral Service, where these Words are, *We shall all be changed in a moment, in the twinkling of an Eye, &c.* the Printer had omitted the *c* in *changed,* and it read thus, *We shall all be hang'd, &c.* [13 March 1729/30]

As earlier, Franklin would raise an issue in an essay or letter then respond to it himself under a different name. In trying to promote a responsible press, he followed an essay on speculative reasoning with an exchange of letters on ghost stories. Unwilling to suspend disbelief, one faux correspondent clinches the debate with an apologue, a comical tale with a point about the value of experience versus authority. On the surface, the tale appears to be a gratuitous joke, but in fact it is essential to making Franklin's point—a hallmark of his comic storytelling.

A certain Curate lived in the Island of Jamaica, who loved his Bottle, no curate better; he chanced to be drinking in a Tavern, when he was called upon to do the last Offices to a Brother departed; upon which with great Reluctance he leaves his Company, but told them he would return immediately: away he hies to the Place of Burial, and, as is usual, reads over the Service for the Dead, 'till he came to the Words, *I heard a Voice from Heaven, saying, blessed, &c.* at which he was interrupted by one of his Companions, who had followed him from the Ale-house, with a "By G—that's a d—'d Lye, for I have been drinking with you all Day at Mother——'s, and if you had heard the Voice, I should have heard it too, for my ears are as good as yours." [23 April 1730]

The masterpiece on the theme of trying to get along with language is an apologue engrained in our culture, concluding the editorial of 10 June 1731. After apologizing for innocently libeling clergy, Franklin demonstrates the futility of trying to please everybody.

A certain well-meaning Man and his Son, were travelling towards a Market Town, with an Ass which they had to sell. The Road was bad; and the old Man therefore rid, but the Son went a-foot.

The first Passenger they met, asked the Father if he was not ashamed to ride by himself, and suffer the poor Lad to wade along thro' the Mire; this induced him to take up his Son behind him: He had not travelled far, when he met others, who said, they were two unmerciful Lubbers to get both on the Back of that poor Ass, in such a deep Road. Upon this the old Man gets off, and let his Son ride alone. The next they met called the Lad a graceless, rascally young Jackanapes, to ride in that Manner thro' the Dirt, while his aged Father trudged along on Foot; and they said the old Man was a Fool, for suffering it. He then bid his Son come down, and walk with him, and they travelle'd on leading the Ass by the Halter; 'till they met another Company, who called them a Couple of senseless Blockheads, for going both on Foot in such a dirty Way, when they had an empty Ass with them, which they might ride upon. The old Man could bear no longer; "My Son,"said he, "it grieves me much that we cannot please all these People: Let us throw the Ass over the next Bridge, and be no farther troubled with him." [10 June 1731]

The clearest advance in comic treatment came in the sort of sketch seen in Silence Dogood or Patience where characters confront us directly. Celia Single and Alice Addertongue reveal themselves by what they say and how they say it, sometimes unaware of what they are revealing. In contrast, Anthony Afterwit's character does not balance comical and invective elements, doubtless because it came too close to Franklin's own experience with parents who tried to trap him into marrying their daughter without a dowry.[10] Afterwit explains how he became saddled with a wife who threatened him with bankruptcy.

I am an honest Tradesman, who never meant Harm to any Body. My Affairs went on smoothly while a Batchelor; but of late I have met with some Difficulties, of which I take the Freedom to give you an Account.

About the Time I first address'd my present Spouse, her Father gave out in Speeches, that if she married a Man he liked, he would give her 200 pounds on the Day of Marriage. 'Tis true he never said so to me, but he always receiv'd me very kindly at his House, and openly countenanc'd my Courtship. I form'd several fine Schemes, what to do with this same 200 pounds and in some Measure neglected my Business on that Account: But unluckily it came to pass, that when the old Gentleman saw I was pretty well engag'd, and that the Match was too far gone to be easily broke off; he, without any Reason given, grew very angry, forbid me the House, and told his Daughter that if she married me he would not give her a Farthing. However (as he foresaw) we were not to be disappointed in that Manner; but having stole a Wedding, I took her home to my House; where we were not in quite so poor a Condition as the Couple describ'd in the Scotch Song, who had

Neither Pot nor Pan,
But four bare Legs together;

for I had a House tolerably furnished, for an ordinary Man, before. No thanks to Dad, who I understand was very much pleased with his politick Management. And I have since learn'd that there are old Curmudgeons (*so called*) besides him, who have this Trick, to marry their Daughters, and yet keep what they might well spare, till they can keep it no longer: But this by way of Digression; *A Word to the Wise is enough.* [10 July 1732]

No sooner settled than Mrs Afterwit begins a train of acquisitions—a looking-glass, table, chairs, china, silver, a maid, clock, "a very fine pacing Mare, which cost 20 pounds."

I could see all along, that this Way of Living was utterly inconsistent with my Circumstances, but had not Resolution enough to help it. Till lately, receiving a very severe Dun, which mention'd the next Court, I began in earnest to project Relief. *Last Monday my Dear went over the River, to see a Relation, and stay a Fortnight, because* she could not bear the Heat of the Town. *In the Interim, I have taken my Turn to make Alterations, viz. I have turn'd away the*

Maid Bag and Baggage (for what should we do with a Maid, who have (except my Boy) none but our selves). I have sold the fine Pacing Mare, and bought a good Milch Cow, with 3 pounds of the Money. I have dispos'd of the Tea-Table, and put a Spinning Wheel in its Place, which methinks looks very pretty: *Nine empty Canisters I have stuff'd with Flax; and with some of the Money of the Tea-Furniture, I have bought a Set of Knitting-Needles; for to tell you a Truth, which I would have go no further, I begin to want Stockings. . . .*

Postscript, You know we can return to our former Way of Living, when we please, if *Dad* will be at the Expence of it. [10 July 1732]

A fortnight later, Celia Single complains about Afterwit's letter with such heat that the editor says he had to censor "Circumstances of her Letter, which point at People *too plainly.*" She warms up by attacking Anthony Afterwit but uses his letter as a springboard for renewing debate on Franklin's editorial policies, complete with stage directions.

I must needs tell you, that some of the Things you print do more Harm than good; particularly I think so of my Neighbour the Tradesman's Letter in one of your late Papers, which has broken the Peace of several Families, by causing Difference between Men and their Wives: I shall give you here one Instance, of which I was an Eye and Ear Witness.

Happening last *Wednesday* Morning to be in at Mrs. *C—ss's*, when her Husband return'd from Market, among other Things which he had bought, he show'd her some Balls of Thread. *My dear,* says he, *I like mightily those Stockings which I yesterday saw Neighbour* Afterwit *knitting for her Husband, of Thread of her own Spinning: I should be glad to have some such Stockins my self; I understand that your Maid Mary is a very good Knitter, and seeing this Thread in Market, I have bought it, that the Girl may make a Pair or two for me.*

Mrs. *Careless* was just then at her Glass, dressing her Head; and turning about with the Pins in her Mouth, *Lord, Child,* says she, *are you crazy? What Time has* Mary *to knit? Who must do the Work, I wonder, if you set her to Knitting?*

Perhaps, my Dear, *says he,* you have a mind to knit 'em yourself; I remember, when I courted you, I once heard you say you had learn'd to knit of your Mother.

I knit Stockins for you, says she, *not I truly; There are poor Women enough in Town that can knit; if you please you may employ them.*

Well, but my dear, *says he,* you know a penny sav'd is a penny got, a pin a day is a groat a year, every little makes a mickle, and there is neither Sin nor Shame in Knitting a pair of Stockins; why should you express such a mighty Aversion to it? As to *poor* Women, you know we are not People of Quality, we have no Income to maintain us, but what arises from my Labour and Industry; methinks you should not be at all displeas'd, if you have an Opportunity to get something as well as my self.

I wonder, says she, *how you can propose such a thing to me; did not you always tell me you would maintain me like a Gentlewoman? If I had married* Capt.——, *he would have scorn'd even to mention Knitting of Stockins.*

Prithee, *says he, (a little nettled)* what do you tell me of your Captains? If you could have had him, I suppose you would; or perhaps you did not very well like him: If I did promise to maintain you like a Gentlewoman, I suppose 'tis time enough for that when you know how to behave like one; mean while 'tis your Duty to help make me able. How long d'ye think I can maintain you at your present Rate of Living?

Pray, says she, (somewhat fiercely, and dashing the Puff into the Powder-Box) *don't use me after this Manner, for I assure you I won't bear it. This is the Fruit of your poison* News-papers; *there shall come no more here, I promise you.*

Bless us, *says he,* what an unaccountable thing is this! Must a Tradesman's Daughter, and the Wife of a Tradesman, necessarily and instantly be a Gentlewoman? You had no Portion; I am forc'd to work for a Living; if you are too great to do the like, there's the Door, go and live upon your Estate, if you can find it; in short, I don't desire to be troubled w'ye.—

What Answer she made, I cannot tell, for knowing that a Man and his Wife are apt to quarrel more violently when before Strangers, than when by themselves, I got up and went out hastily: But I understood from *Mary,* who came to me of an Errand in the Evening, that they dined together pretty peaceably, (the Balls of Thread that had caused the Difference, being thrown into the Kitchen Fire) of which I was very glad to hear.

I have several times in your Paper seen severe Reflections upon us Women, for Idleness and Extravagance, but I do not remember to have once seen any such Animadversions upon the Men. If I were dispos'd to be censorious, I could furnish you with Instances enough: I might mention Mr. *Billiard* who spends more than he earns, at the Green Table; and would have been in jail long since, were it not for his industrious Wife: Mr. *Husselcap,* who often all day long leaves his Business for the rattling of Halfpence in a certain Alley: Mr. *Finikin,* who has seven different Suits of fine Cloaths, and wears a Change every Day, while his Wife and Children sit at home half naked; Mr *Crownhim,* who is always dreaming over the Chequer-board, and cares not how the World goes, so he gets the Game; Mr. *T'otherpot* the Tavern-haunter; Mr. *Bookish,* the everlasting Reader; Mr. *Tweedledum,* Mr. *Toot-a-toot,* and several others, who are mighty diligent at any thing besides their Business. I say, if I were dispos'd to be censorious, I might mention all these, and more; but I hate to be thought a Scandalizer of my neighbours, and therefore forbear. And for your part, I would advise you, for the future, to entertain your Readers with something else besides People's Reflections upon one another; for remember, that there are Holes enough to be pick'd in your Coat as well as others; and those that are affronted by the Satyrs you may publish, will not consider so much who *wrote,* as who *printed.* [24 July 1732]

In mid-August, the competing *Mercury* printed a long poem from a London weekly on a day in the life of a modern woman, including the tea-table's gossip—"Their Innuendo's, Hints and Slanders/Their Meanings lew'd, and double Entanders." Franklin's *Gazette* replied by praising gossip (read libel and slander) as "a Virtue" that moderates folly and vice. His next issue dramatized the point as Alice Addertongue displays what Jonathan Swift's *Tale of a Tub* called "the mechanical Operation of the Spirit," unencumbered by moral or ethical values, as when Swift's narrator says, "Last Week I saw a Woman *flay'd,* and you will hardly believe, how much it altered her Person for the worse."[11] This sort of anesthetized sensibility will surface repeatedly in Franklin's satires.

I am a young Girl of about thirty-five, and live at present with my Mother. I have no Care upon my Head of getting a Living, and therefore find it my Duty as well as Inclination to exercise my Talent at *Censure,* for the Good of my Country folks. There was, I am told, a certain generous Emperor, who if a Day had passed over his Head, in which he had conferred no benefit on any man, used to say to his Friends, in Latin, *Diem perdidi,* that is, it seems, *I have lost a Day.* I believe I should make use of the same Expression, if it were possible for a Day to pass in which I had not, or miss'd, an Opportunity to scandalize somebody: But, Thanks be praised, no such Misfortune has befel me these dozen Years.

Yet, whatever Good I may do, I cannot pretend that I entred into the Practice of this Virtue from a principle of Publick Spirit; for I remember that when a Child, I had a violent Inclination to be ever talking in my own Praise, and being continually told that it was ill Manners, and once severely whipt for it, the confin'd Stream form'd itself a new Channel, and I began to speak for the future in the Dispraise of others. This I found more agreable to Company, and almost as much so to my self: For what great Difference can there be, between putting your self up, or putting your Neighbour down? *Scandal,* like other Virtues, is in part its own Reward, as it gives us the Satisfaction of making our selves appear better than others, or others no better than ourselves.

My Mother, good Woman, and I, have heretofore differ'd upon this Account. She argu'd that Scandal spoilt all good Conversation, and I insisted that without it there could be no such Thing. Our Disputes once rose so high, that we parted Tea-Table, and I concluded to entertain my Acquaintance in the Kitchin. The first

Day of this Separation we both drank Tea at the same Time, but she with her Visitors in the Parlor. She would not hear of the least Objection to anyone's Character, but began a new sort of Discourse in some such queer philosophical Manner as this; *I am mightily pleas'd sometimes,* says she, *when I observe and consider that the World is not so bad as People out of humour imagine it to be. There is something amiable, some good Quality or other in every body. . . .* I peep'd in at the Door, and never in my Life before saw such a Set of simple vacant Countenances; they look'd somehow neither glad, nor sorry, nor angry, nor pleas'd, nor indifferent, nor attentive; but (excuse the Simile) like so many blue wooden Images of Rie Doe.

I in the Kitchin had already begun a ridiculous Story of Mr.——'s Intrigue with his Maid, and his Wife's Behaviour upon the Discovery; at some Passages we laugh'd heartily, and one of the gravest of Mama's Company, without making any Answer to her Discourse, got up *to go and see what the Girls were so merry about:* and she was follow'd by a Second, and shortly after by a Third, till at last the old Gentlewoman found herself quite alone, and being convinc'd that her Project was impracticable, came her self and finish'd her Tea with us; ever since which *Saul also has been among the Prophets* [1 *Samuel* 10:11; i.e., she's a changed person], and our Disputes lie dormant.

By Industry and Application, I have made my self the Center of all the *Scandal* in the Province, there is little flirting but I hear of it. I began the World with this Maxim, *That no Trade can subsist without Returns;* and accordingly, whenever I receiv'd a good Story, I endeavour'd to give two or a better in the Room of it. My Punctuality in this Way of Dealing gave such Encouragement, that it has procur'd me an incredible deal of Business, which without Diligence and good Method it would be impossible for me to go through. For besides the Stock of Defamation thus naturally flowing upon me, I practice an Art by which I can pump Scandal out of People that are the least enclin'd that way. Shall I discover my Secret? Yes; to let it die with me would be inhuman.—

If I have never heard Ill of some Person, I always impute it to defective Intelligence; *for there are none without their Faults, no not one.* If she is a Woman, I take the first Opportunity to let all her Acquaintance know I have heard that one of the handsomest or best Men in Town has said something in Praise either of her Beauty, her Wit, her Virtue, or her good Management. If you know any thing about Humane Nature, you perceive that this naturally introduces a Conversation turning upon all her Failings, past, present, and to come. To the same purpose, and with the same Success, I cause every Man of Reputation to be praised before his Competitors in Love, Business, or Esteem on Account of any particular Qualification.

Near the Times of *Election,* if I find it necessary, I commend every candidate before some of the opposite Party, listning attentively to what is said of him in answer: (But Commendations in this latter case are not always necessary, and should be used judiciously;) of late Years I needed only observe what they said of one another freely; and having for the Help of Memory taken Account of all Informations & Accusations received, whoever peruses my Writings after my Death, may happen to think, that during a certain Term, the People of *Pennsylvania* chose into all their Offices of Honour and Trust, the veriest Knaves, Fools and Rascals in the whole Province. The Time of Election used to be a busy Time with me, but this Year, with Concern I speak it, People are grown so good natur'd, so intent upon mutual Feasting and friendly Entertainment, that I see no prospect of much Employment from that Quarter.

I mention'd above, that without good Method I could not go thro' my Business: In my Father's Life-time I had some Instruction in Accompts, which I now apply with Advantage to my own Affairs. I keep a regular Set of Books, and can tell at an Hour's Warning how it stands between me and the World. In my *Daybook* I enter every Article of Defamation as it is transacted; for Scandals *receiv'd in,* I give Credit; and when I pay them out again, I make the Persons, to whom they respectively relate *Debtor.* In my *Journal,* I add to each Story by Way of Improvement, such probable Circumstance as I think it will bear, and in my *Ledger* the whole is regularly posted.

I suppose the Reader already condemns me in his Heart, for this particular of *adding Circumstances;* but I justify that part of my Practice thus. 'Tis a Principle with me, that none ought to have a greater Share of Reputation than they really deserve; if they have, 'tis an Imposition upon the Publick: I know it is every one's Interest, and therefore believe they endeavour, to conceal *all* their Vices and Follies; and I hold, that those People are *extraordinary* foolish or careless who suffer a *Fourth* of their Failings to come to publick Knowledge: Taking then the common Prudence and Imprudence of Mankind in a Lump, I suppose none suffer above *one Fifth* to be discovered: Therefore when I hear of any person's Misdoing, I think I keep within Bounds if in relating it I only make it *three times* worse than it is; and I reserve to my self the Privilege of charging them with one Fault in four, which, for aught I know, they may be entirely innocent of. You see there are but few so careful of doing Justice as my self; what Reason then have Mankind to complain of *Scandal?* In a general way, the worst that is said of us is only half what *might* be said, if all our Faults were seen.

But alas, two great Evils have lately befaln me at the same time; an extream Cold that I can scarce speak, and a most terrible Toothach that I dare hardly open my Mouth: For some Days past I have receiv'd ten Stories for one I have paid; and I am not able to ballance my Accounts without your Assistance. I have long thought that if you would make your Paper a Vehicle of Scandal, you would double the Number of your Subscribers. I send you herewith Account of 4 *Knavish Tricks,* 2 *crackt M[aide]n[hea]ds,* 5 *Cu[cko]ld[o]ms,* 3 *drub'd Wives,* and 4 *Henpeck'd Husbands,* all within this Fortnight; which you may, as Articles of News, deliver to the Publick; and if my Toothach continues, shall send you more.

[Adds the editor:] I thank my Correspondent Mrs. Addertongue for her Good-Will; but desire to be excus'd inserting the Articles of News she has sent me; such Things being in Reality *no News at all.* [12 September 1732]

In the first few years with his own business, Franklin depended on comic material to defend against critics and attract readers. In having to fill columns each week, he had earlier acquired valuable experience in modeling the material to popular taste for the *Spectator* or the various works of Daniel Defoe. Now he adapted dramatic technique from the London theater and from a new model, the satires of Jonathan Swift. Besides the shift to a style more dramatically immediate, Franklin's concern shifted from the genteel social comedy of Addison and Steele to the moral issues of Jonathan Swift relating particularly to self-delusion as a consequence of misusing and abusing reason. Swift described it thus: "When a Man's Fancy gets *astride* on his Reason, when Imagination is at Cuffs with the Senses, and common Understanding, as well as common Sense is Kickt out of Doors," the consequence is "a perpetual Possession of being well Deceived."[12] Franklin would play variations on the theme of deception—deception of others and of oneself—ever after.

3

Philadelphia's Poor Richard

1733–1748

In adopting the model of Swift's satire, Franklin used techniques familiar from his own practice of Socratic irony by pretending to be innocent or ignorant. He pretended to be madcap Poor Richard Saunders so successfully that the popular imagination confused worldly Franklin with Poor Richard as the Polonius of puritanical proverbs. In a day when a printer needed an almanac to stay in business, Poor Richard gave Franklin the edge in competition. Where the *Pennsylvania Gazette* aimed at informing and amusing a developing class of newspaper-reading Americans, Poor Richard's almanac catered to those who never read anything else. They needed calendars and such essential information as seasons, moon- and sunsets, tides, and court dates. The information was common to all regional almanacs, so Franklin's problem was to print an almanac more attractive than a half-dozen others in Philadelphia.

In December 1732, at a modest five pence a copy, he introduced *Poor Richard, an Almanack for the Year of Christ 1733* (almanacs usually appeared in October for the following year). Just as he had imitated popular comic models to beat competition from Samuel Keimer's newspaper, Franklin imitated models already proven popular with an array of familiar comic features. The title itself fused titles of three models. It echoed Newport, Rhode

Island's almanac, *Poor Robin,* printed by his brother James Franklin, who took the title from London's best-selling comic almanac.[1] Spreading his net, Benjamin Franklin also adopted the London *Poor Robin's* facetious character and took the family name of a third model—Richard Saunder (no "s"), another popular London almanac maker who promoted scientific astronomy as antidote to superstitious astrology. By 1732, however, Saunder had been reduced to arguing that lightning bolts were not boulders and that the heavens did not rain frogs. Franklin's eclectic Richard Saunders became the distinctive comic voice of America—exuberant, irreverent, both deluding and self-deluded.

Over a thousand copies of Franklin's first edition sold out in two days.[2] Five years later, he would sell more than three thousand copies outside of Philadelphia. Eventually sales would peak at ten thousand copies annually, generating about a third of Franklin's income.[3]

Franklin filled the almanac's empty spaces with proverbs containing "the Wisdom of many Ages and Nations."[4] His principal resource was a dictionary compiled by James Howell of proverbs in French, Spanish, and even Welsh, translated and explained in English prose and verse in parallel columns and arranged in several categories for easy reference.[5] Franklin's selection from Howell's proverbs apparently was dictated by available space in *Poor Richard's Almanac,* but not at the expense of style. He would sharpen the point of each one, clarify the sense, or distill the essence as in these random samples (with Howell's proverbs given here in parentheses and cross-referenced to the almanac as *PRA*).

—*(A Ship under sayl, a man in compleat Armour, a Woman with a great belly, are three of the handsomest sights.—Spanish, p. 8)*[6]

A Ship under sail and a big-bellied Woman, Are the handsomest two things that can be seen common.—*PRA,* June 1735

—(*Two may keep Counsel when one is away.—English, 19)*

Three may keep a Secret, if two of them are dead.—*PRA*, July 1735

—(*Who goeth to School to himselfe, may find a fool to his Master.—English, 19)*

He that teaches himself, hath a fool for his master.—*PRA, January 1741*

Sometimes Franklin would update the diction or make the allusions more homely to sharpen the humor, as in:

—(*A Client twixt his Attorney and Counsellor, is like a Goose twixt two Foxes.—English, 9)*

A countryman between two Lawyers, is like a fish between two cats.—*PRA*, February 1737

—(*The Fox who sleeps in the Morning hath not his tongue feathered.—French, 7)*

The sleeping Fox catches no poultry.—*PRA*, September 1743

—(*When the mouth is shut, flies cannot enter.—Spanish, 2)*

The close mouth catches no flies.—*PRA*, February 1742

—(*Who hath a glass roof of his own, let him not throw stones at his neighbours.—Spanish, 11)*

Don't throw stones at your neighbours, if your own windows are glass.—*PRA*, August 1736

—(There are more old good fellows, then old Physicians.—French, 4)

There's more old Drunkards than old Doctors.—*PRA,* April 1736

Given alternative versions of the same proverb, Franklin would choose the one more universally applicable. Faced with "He who liveth in hope doth dance in a hoope" (Italian, 5) and "He who lives by hope, dies farting" (Italian, 13), he chose the latter (February 1736). His final almanac, now called *Poor Richard Improved,* would sanitize the same proverb.

He that lives upon Hope will die fasting. (February 1758)

Franklin's style is best appreciated compared with that of Titan Leeds, his chief competitor, who rendered proverbs in doggerel couplets: "Out of the Frying into the Fire/And he that's not True must be a Lyar" (January 1730), or "Take my advice, & go to Bed/ And be content with whom thou'rt wed" (December 1730). Leeds also prefaced his almanacs with awkward doggerel, as in justifying switching printers from Samuel Keimer to Andrew Bradford in 1731: "Many people do me blame/My Printer for to change,/ But I do not think it so,/For all the World's the same." Even his prose proved convoluted—"My Calculations may be as true as others, though some object against it, without giving any Reason, or shewing wherein I have been wrong; until they do that I will not believe them, nor Men of Sense will not neither" (*American Almanac,* 1731). What satirist could resist so tempting a target?

At Poor Richard's debut, Titan Leeds' *American Almanac* trafficed in old-fashioned astrology, making Leeds vulnerable to both parody of his style and burlesque of his substance. Franklin even burlesqued Leeds's "Catalogue of Principal Kings" to introduce Poor Richard as "an American Prince, without Subjects, his Wife being Viceroy over him."

With an initial boost from mocking Titan Leeds, Franklin would produce twenty-six consecutive almanacs, several with comical prefaces by Poor Richard and one by a surprise guest. His first preface followed a by-then popular comic convention of claiming a popular astrologer was dead. Self-promoting seventeenth-century almanac maker John Partridge had a devoted following until 1708, when Jonathan Swift, pretending to be fellow astrologer Isaac Bickerstaff, announced the living Partridge's death: "I can prove, not only by my Rules, but those of *Abul Pharage*, that he dy'd exactly at the Time foretold. His Burial . . . was kept Secret, to ruin my Reputation."[7] Partridge repeatedly advertised that Bickerstaff had miscalculated the figures and that Partridge was alive and well and living in London. Thereafter, parodying Partridge became an international sport. Almanacs appeared even after his well-publicized death in 1715 as coming from beyond the grave. By 1732, he was ripe for transplanting in America as Titan Leeds in Poor Richard Saunders's first introductory preface. Franklin also introduces as coming attractions an internal triangle, the protagonists in the prefaces to come—Poor Richard and his wife Bridget—along with the shadowy figure called "the Printer." The voice that at first echoes conventional comic almanacs will soon acquire Poor Dick's own timbre.

Courteous Reader,

I might in this place attempt to gain thy Favour, by declaring that I write Almanacks with no other View than that of the publick Good; but in this I should not be sincere; and Men are now adays too wise to be deceiv'd by Pretences how specious soever. The plain Truth of the Matter is, I am excessive poor, and my Wife, good Woman, is, I tell her, excessive proud; she cannot bear, she says, to sit spinning in her Shift of Tow, while I do nothing but gaze at the Stars; and has threatned more than once to burn all my Books and Rattling-Traps (as she calls my Instruments) if I do not make some profitable Use of them for the good of my Family. The Printer has offer'd me some considerable share of the Profits, and I have thus begun to comply with my Dame's desire.

Indeed this Motive would have had Force enough to have made me publish an Almanack many Years since, had it not been overpower'd by my Regard for my good Friend and Fellow-

Student, Mr. *Titan Leeds,* whose Interest I was extreamly unwilling to hurt: But this Obstacle (I am far from speaking it with Pleasure) is soon to be removed, since inexorable Death, who was never known to respect Merit, has already prepared the mortal Dart, the fatal Sister has already extended her destroying Shears, and that ingenious Man must soon be taken from us. He dies, by my Calculation made at his Request, on *Oct. 17, 1733.* 3 ho. 29 min. P.M. at the very Instant of the Conjunction of the Moon and Mercury: By his own Calculation he will survive till the 26th of the same Month. This small difference between us we have disputed whenever we have met these 9 Years past; but at length he is inclinable to agree with my Judgment; Which of us is most exact, a little Time will now determine. As therefore these Provinces may no longer expect to see any of his Performances after this Year, I think my self free to take up the Task, and request a share of the publick Encouragement; which I am the more apt to hope for on this Account, that the Buyer of my Almanack may consider himself, not only as purchasing an useful Utensil, but as performing an Act of Charity, to his poor *Friend and Servant* R. Saunders. [*PRA,* 1733]

Incredibly, Titan Leeds leaped to the bait. His next almanac floundered with complaints against "this precise Predicter who predicts to a Minute" for falsely claiming that Leeds calculated the date of his own death: "I do not pretend to that knowledge, altho' he has usurpt the knowledge of the Almighty herein, and manifested himself a Fool and a Liar."[8] As Poor Richard constructs his own character, he continues to undermine Leeds's credibility.

Courteous Readers,

Your kind and charitable Assistance last Year, in purchasing so large an Impression of my Almanacks, has made my Circumstances much more easy in the World, and requires my grateful Acknowledgment. My Wife has been enabled to get a Pot of her own, and is no longer oblig'd to borrow one from a Neighbour; nor have we ever since been without something of our own to put in it. She has also got a pair of Shoes, two new Shifts, and a new warm Petticoat; and for my part, I have bought a second-hand Coat, so good, that I am now not asham'd to go to Town or be seen there. These Things have render'd her Temper so much more pacifick than it us'd to be, that I may say, I have slept more, and more quietly within this last Year, than in the three foregoing Years put together. Accept my hearty Thanks therefor, and my sincere Wishes for your Health and Prosperity.

In the Preface to my last Almanack, I foretold the Death of my dear old Friend and Fellow-Student, the learned and ingenious Mr. *Titan Leeds,* which was to be on the 17th of *October, 1733,* 3 h. 29 m P.M. at the very instant of the Conjunction of the Moon and Mercury. By his own Calculation he was to survive till the 26th of the same Month, and expire in the Time of the Eclipse, near 11 a clock, A.M. At which of these Times he died, or whether he be really yet dead, I cannot at this present Writing positively assure my Readers; forasmuch as a Disorder in my own Family demanded my Presence, and would not permit me as I had intended, to be with him in his last Moments, to receive his last Embrace, to close his Eyes, and do the Duty of a Friend in performing the last Offices to the Departed. Therefore it is that I cannot positively affirm whether he be dead or not; for the Stars only show to the Skilful, what will happen in the natural and universal Chain of Causes and Effects; but 'tis well known, that the Events which would otherwise certainly happen at certain Times in the Course of Nature, are sometimes set aside or postpon'd for wise and good Reasons, by the immediate particular Dispositions of Providence; which particular Dispositions the Stars can by no Means discover or foreshow. There is, however, (and I cannot speak it without Sorrow) there is the strongest Probability that my dear Friend is *no more;* for there appears in his Name, as I am assured, an Almanack for the Year 1734, in which I am treated in a very gross and unhandsome Manner; in which I am called *a false Predicter, an Ignorant, a conceited Scribbler, a Fool, and a Lyar.* Mr. *Leeds* was too well bred to use any Man so indecently and so scurrilously, and moreover his Esteem and Affection for me was extraordinary: So that it is to be feared, that Pamphlet may be only a contrivance of somebody or other, who hopes perhaps to sell two or three Year's Almanacks still, by the sole Force and Virtue of Mr. *Leeds's* Name; but certainly, to put Words into the Mouth of a Gentleman and a Man of Letters, against his Friend, which the meanest and most scandalous of the People might be asham'd to utter even in a drunken Quarrel, is an unpardonable Injury to his Memory, and an Imposition upon the Publick. [*PRA*, 1734]

> Leeds could not leave well enough alone. He reacted in his preface for 1735: "I shall say little more about it than, as a Friend, to advise he will never take upon him to predict or ascribe any Persons Death, till he has learned to do it better."[9] Having delayed until Leeds had spoken, Poor Richard responded with an exuberant preface. Besides adapting Swift's technique of accepting the premises of his victim's argument then taking them to their absurd conclusion with a straight face, Franklin was also revealing how Poor Dick's deception of Leeds was leading to his own self-delusion, even to using Latin tags that were out of keeping with his character.

Whatever may be the Musick of the Spheres, how great soever the Harmony of the Stars, 'tis certain there is no Harmony among the Stargazers; but they are perpetually growling and snarling at one another like strange Curs, or like some Men at their Wives: I had resolved to keep the Peace on my own part and affront none of them; and I shall persist in that Resolution: But having receiv'd much Abuse from *Titan Leeds* deceas'd, (*Titan Leeds* when living would not have us'd me so!) I say, having receiv'd much Abuse from the Ghost of *Titan Leeds,* who pretends to be still living, and to write Almanacks in spight of me and my Predictions, I cannot help saying, that tho' I take it patiently, I take it very unkindly. And whatever he may pretend, 'tis undoubtedly true that he is really defunct and dead. First because the Stars are seldom disappointed, never but in the Case of Men, *Sapiens dominabitur astris [the wise will be ruled by the stars],* and they foreshow'd his Death at the Time I predicted it. Secondly, 'Twas requisite and necessary he should die punctually at that Time, for the Honour of Astrology, the Art professed both by him and his Father before him. Thirdly, 'tis plain to every one that reads his two last Almanacks (for 1734 and 1735) that they are not written with that *Life* his Performances use to be written with; the Wit is low and flat, the little Hints dull and spiritless, nothing smart in them but *Hudibras's* Verses against Astrology at the Head of the Months in the last, which no Astrologer but a *dead one* would have inserted, and no Man *living* would or could write such Stuff as the rest. But lastly, I shall convince him from his own Words, that he is dead, *ex ore suo condemnatus est [he is condemned out of his own mouth]* for in his Preface to his Almanack for 1734, he says *"Saunders adds another* ***Gross Falshood*** *in his Almanack,* viz. *that by my own Calculation I shall* survive *until the* 26th *of the said Month October* 1733*, which is as* untrue *as the former."* Now if it be, as *Leeds* says, *untrue* and a *gross Falshood* that he surviv'd till the 26th of October 1733, then it is certainly *true* that he died *before* that Time: And if he died before that Time, he is dead now, to all Intents and Purposes, any thing he may say to the contrary notwithstanding. And at what Time before the 26th is it so likely he should die, as at the Time by me predicted, *viz.* the 17th of October aforesaid? But if some People will walk and be troublesome after Death, it may perhaps be born with a little, because it cannot well be avoided unless one would be at the Pains and Expence of laying them in the *Red Sea;* however, they should not presume too much upon the Liberty allow'd them; I know Confinement must needs be mighty irksome to the free Spirit of an Astronomer, and I am too compassionate to proceed suddenly to Extremities with it; nevertheless, tho' I resolve with Reluctance, I shall not long defer, if it does not speedily learn to treat its living Friends with better Manners. [*PRA*, 1735]

For the 1736 preface, Poor Richard played the biter-bit victim, claiming to be attacked as he had attacked Leeds and incidentally disclaiming identity with Benjamin Franklin—which contemporaries would have taken as ludicrous.[10] Franklin had become vulnerable after engaging the Presbyterian establishment in controversy by defending Rev. Samuel Hemphill's popular sermons despite their having been plagiarized. As Franklin himself became fair game for pamphleteers, Poor Richard, who had so well helped build the Printer's reputation, now turned to preserve it but at the cost of losing his own humorous edge.

Loving Readers . . . The general Approbation you have been so good as to favour me with, has excited the Envy of some, and drawn upon me the Malice of others. These Ill-willers of mine, despited at the great Reputation I gain'd by exactly predicting another Man's Death, have endeavour'd to deprive me of it all at once in the most effectual Manner, by reporting that I my self was never alive. They say in short, *That there is no such Man as I am;* and have spread this Notion so thoroughly in the Country, that I have been frequently told it to my Face by those that don't know me. This is not civil Treatment, to endeavour to deprive me of my very Being, and reduce me to a Non-entity in the Opinion of the publick. But so long as I know my self to walk about, eat, drink and sleep, I am satisfied that *there is really such a Man as I am,* whatever they may say to the contrary: And the World may be satisfied likewise; for if there were no such Man as I am, how is it possible I should appear publickly to hundreds of People, as I have done for several Years past, in print? I need not, indeed, have taken any Notice of so idle a Report, if it had not been for the sake of my Printer, to whom my Enemies are pleased to ascribe my Productions; and who it seems is as unwilling to father my Offspring, as I am to lose the Credit of it: Therefore to clear him entirely, as well as to vindicate my own Honour, I make this publick and serious Declaration, which I desire may be believed, to wit, *That what I have written heretofore, and do now write, neither was nor is written by any other Man or Men, Person or Persons whatsoever.* Those who art not satisfied with this, must needs be very unreasonable. [*PRA*, 1736]

Franklin further dampened Poor Dick's comical exuberance the next year. Competitors seem to have accepted Poor Richard's carping good-naturedly, but in 1737 he took on a new antagonist, almanac maker John Jerman. Jerman, a leading Welsh Quaker, was a reputable mathematician who prefaced his almanacs with deeply religious verses. By also carrying on the tradition of fail-safe prognostication popular in Welsh almanacs,[11] Jerman left himself open to Poor Dick's parody.

As to the Weather, if I were to fall into the Method my Brother *J——n* sometimes uses, and tell you, *Snow here or in New England,—Rain here or in South-Carolina,—Cold to the Northward,—Warm to the Southward,* and the like, whatever Errors I might commit, I should be something more secure of not being detected in them: But I consider, it will be of no Service to any body to know what Weather it is 1000 miles off, and therefore I always set down positively what Weather my Reader will have, be he where he will at the time . . . and if it does not come to pass accordingly, let the Fault be laid upon the Printer, who, 'tis very like, may have transpos'd or misplac'd it, perhaps for the Conveniency of putting in his Holidays: And since, in spight of all I can say, People will give him great part of the Credit of making my Almanacs, 'tis but reasonable he should take some of the Blame.

As "Philomath" in the *Pennsylvania Gazette,* 20 October 1737, Franklin used the same direct, bitter sarcasm against obtuse entries in Leeds's 1736 almanac: "May 21 *The Sword of Satan is drawn.* June 7. *The Cat eat the Candle.* Now, Sir, why should the Sword of Satan be drawn to kill the Cat on the 21st Day of *May,* when it plainly appears in Print, that the Cat did not eat the Candle till the 7th of *June* following? This Question no Man but an Astrologer can possibly answer." At the end of Poor Richard's preface for 1737, however, as if Franklin's outbursts had proven cathartic, he reprised the preface of 1733 in attempting to recover Poor Richard's comical personality.

If the generous Purchaser of my Labours could see how often his *Five pence* helps to light up the comfortable Fire, line the Pot, fill the Cup and make glad the Heart of a poor Man and an honest good old Woman, he would not think his Money ill laid out, tho' the Almanack of his *Friend and Servant* R. Saunders were one half blank Paper. [*PRA*, 1737]

To help restore his earlier comic detachment, Franklin recruited a surprise surrogate, "Your loving Friend, Bridget Saunders." To the independent spirit of Silence Dogood she brought a bewitching drollery expressed in a dramatic monologue in sharp contrast to Poor Dick's recent rants.

My good Man set out last Week for *Potowmack,* to visit an old Stargazer of his Acquaintance, and see about a little Place for us to settle and end our Days on. He left the Copy of his Almanack seal'd up, and bid me send it to the Press. I suspected something, and therefore as soon as he was gone, I open'd it, to see if he had not been flinging some of his old Skitts at me. Just as I thought, so it was. And truly, (for want of somewhat else to say, I suppose) he had put into his Preface, that his Wife *Bridget*—was this, and that, and t'other.—What a peasecods! Cannot I have a little Fault or two, but all the Country must see it in print! They have already been told, at one time that I am proud, another time that I am loud, and that I have got a new Petticoat, and abundance of such kind of stuff; and now, forsooth! all the World must know, that *Poor Dick's* Wife has lately taken a fancy to drink a little Tea now and then. A mighty matter, truly, to make a Song of! 'Tis true; I had a little Tea of a Present from the Printer last Year; and what, must a body throw it away? In short, I thought the Preface was not worth a printing, and so I fairly scratch'd it all out, and I believe you'll like our Almanack never the worse for it.

Upon looking over the Months, I see he has put in abundance of foul Weather this Year; and therefore I have scatter'd here and there, where I could find room, some *fair, pleasant, sunshiny, &c.* for the Good-Women to dry their Clothes in. If it does not come to pass according to my Desire, I have shown my Good-will, however; and I hope they'll take it in good part.

I had a Design to make some other Corrections; and particularly to change some of the Verses that I don't very well like; but I have just now unluckily broke my Spectacles; which obliges me to give it you as it is. [*PRA*, 1738]

Unable or unwilling to sustain her lively spirit, Poor Richard returned the next year with renewed sarcasm in parodying John Jerman's diagram of the heavens as a house inhabited by personified signs of the Zodiac.

Ignorant Men wonder how we Astrologers foretell Weather so exactly, unless we deal with the old black Devil. Alas! 'tis as easy as pissing abed. For Instance; The Stargazer peeps at the Heavens thro' a long Glass: He sees perhaps **Taurus**, or the great Bull, in a mighty Chase, stamping on the Floor of his House, swinging his Tail about . . . there you have Wind and Thunder. He spies perhaps **Virgo** (or the Virgin); she turns her Head round as it were to see if any body observ'd her; then crouching down gently, with her Hands on her Knees, she looks wistfully for a while right forward. He judges rightly what she's about: And having calculated the Distance and allow'd Time for it's Falling, finds that next Spring we shall have a fine *April* shower. What can be more natural than this? I might instance the like in many other particulars; but this may be sufficient to prevent our being taken for Conjurors. O the wonderful Knowledge to be found in the Stars! Even the smallest Things are written there, if you had but Skill to read: When my Brother *J—m-n* erected a Scheme to know which was best for his sick Horse, to sup a new-laid Egg, or a little Broth, he found that the Stars plainly gave their Verdict for Broth, and the Horse sup'd his Broth; Now, what do you think became of the Horse? You shall know in my next.

Then, abruptly, halfway through the 1739 preface, Poor Richard declared that the almanac would henceforth treat morality and religion. The new policy coincided with the visit to America of the celebrated evangelist George Whitfield, who, aided and abetted by Franklin's press, would ignite the first Great Awakening throughout the colonies.[12] At this time, Franklin also engaged in local controversy against Pennsylvania's proprietors' refusal to pay a fair share of taxes, the Quaker establishment's pacifism in the face of impending threats from invasion, and Bradford's plans to publish the *American Magazine* to counter Franklin's plans for publishing the *General Magazine* in January 1740.

Besides the usual Things expected in an Almanac, I hope the profess'd Teachers of Mankind will excuse my scattering here and there some instructive Hints in Matters of Morality and Religion. And be not thou disturbed, O grave and sober Reader, if among the many serious Sentences in my Book, thou findest me trifling now and then, and talking idly . . . The Vain Youth that reads my Almanack for the sake of an idle Joke, will perhaps meet with a serious Reflection, that he may ever after be the better for. [*PRA*, 1739]

Naturally Poor Richard's humor ebbed and flowed with eddies and currents in Franklin's life. As Philadelphia postmaster since 1737, he was accused of blocking Bradford's newspaper from the mails. As clerk and printer for the legislature, he faced political enemies.[13] As a Mason, Franklin's liberal religious views reached his parents at Boston, requiring filial reassurance. Even success had liabilities. His almanac's circulation spread to reach more readers but at greater distances, requiring Franklin to rely more on universal homilies than local howlers. Exploiting the Great Awakening would explain the shift to moral values but not the decompression of the comic spirit. Reverting to a dream vision, Poor Richard's preface for 1740 revealed the fragility of Franklin's sense of humor. Maybe he thought everyone would blame the dramatized ghost of Titan Leeds for outrageously libeling devout Quaker John Jerman as a closet Catholic and moralist William Birkett, a philomath loyal to Bradford, as a confirmed drunk. The ghost sends Poor Richard a message.

The People of this Infidel Age, perhaps, will hardly believe this Story. But you may give them these three Signs by which they shall be convinc'd of the Truth of it. About the middle of June *next,* J. J——n *Philomat, shall be openly reconciled to the* Church of Rome, *and give all his Goods and Chattles to the Chappel, being perverted by a certain* Country Schoolmaster. *On the 7th of* September *following my old Friend* W. B——t *shall be sober 9 Hours to the Astonishment of all his Neighbours: And about the same time* W.B. *and* A.B. *will publish another Almanack in my Name, in spight of Truth and Common Sense.* [*PRA,* 1740]

Perhaps sensing that he had mistaken invective for irony, Franklin's *Pennsylvania Gazette* (24 July 1740) commented, "Where Invectives are contain'd in any Piece, there is no good-natur'd Printer but had much rather be employ'd in Work of another kind." William Birkett, who usually used his prefaces to teach lessons in astronomy, prefaced *Poor Will* for 1741 by warning youth to be wary of a "witty and deceitful" person "discerning nothing but himself . . . a debauched Person, much given to the Flesh, constant to neither Wife nor Mistress." Jerman's preface that same year decried Franklin directly: "His false Prophesy concerning me . . . is altogether false and untrue; which is evidently known to all that know me, and plainly shews, that he is one of Baal's false Prophets." Poor Richard in 1741 offered no preface at all. His next complained against critics who persisted in denying his existence.

Who knows him? they cry; *Where does he live?*—But what is that to them? If I delight in a private Life, have they any Right to drag me out of my Retirement? I have good Reasons for concealing the Place of my Abode. 'Tis time for an old Man, as I am, to think of preparing for his great Remove. . . . I have had enough of 'em. All that these angry Folks can say, will never provoke me to tell them where I live. I would eat my Nails first. [*PRA,* 1742]

His last paragraph unloads invective on John Jerman for calling Poor Richard "one of Baals' false prophets." Jerman was not going to take it anymore. He identified "R—S—rs" as "B—F—n" and announced that, having been Franklin's customer, he was taking his printing business elsewhere.[14] Poor Richard's preface for 1743 did not react but consisted entirely of instructions in winemaking. The year's humor consisted of three literary anecdotes at the end, one in verse about how the man and his son in trying to please everyone lost their ass. In 1744 he again pursued Jerman relentlessly, mocking his complaints—"I think such Language between old Men and Scholars unbecoming" (*PRA,* 1744)—and the following year, he devoted the preface to explaining astrological signs seriously. Finally, as either resignation or a declaration of independence, the entire preface of 1746 loosely imitated John Dryden's translation of Virgil's *Georgics* on the joys of a rural retreat.

Who is *Poor Richard?* People oft enquire,
Where lives? What is he?—never yet the nigher.
Somewhat to ease your Curiositie,
Take these slight Sketches of my Dame and me.
Thanks to kind Readers and a careful Wife.
With Plenty bless'd, I lead an easy Life;
My Business Writing; hers to drain the Mead,
Or crown the barren Hill with useful Shade . . .
Our Table neat, Meals temperate; and our Door
Op'ning spontaneous to the bashful Poor.
Free from the bitter Rage of Party Zeal,
All those we love who seek the publick Weal . . .
Our Souls sincere, our Purpose fair and free,
Without Vain Glory or Hypocrisy:
Than[k]ful if well; if ill, we kiss the Rod;
Resign with Hope, and put our Trust in **God.** [*PRA,* 1746]

Franklin had recently moved to a larger house near center city. To call it a bucolic retreat was ludicrous. But the praise of retirement was prescient. In twenty years, he had built a very profitable business that included partnerships with former apprentices up and down the seaboard. In 1748, he could afford to retire at age forty-two. Obsessed by electrical experiments at home and enmeshed in political activities, he found David Hall a suitable partner to manage the business. Hall would manage very well. He would send Franklin an average of (in today's money) $30,000 the first nine years after Franklin retired.[15] Old grumpy Poor Richard, all passion spent after fifteen years, almost retired with him.

4

Philadelphia Comic Relief

1748–1757

Although strained over the years, the humor of *Poor Richard's* prefaces helped create the public taste for an indigenous comic hero. Franklin's more serious writing led to increasing success in business, technology, and public service. He wrote position papers for the Pennsylvania legislature (*Nature and Necessity of a Paper Currency*) and instructions for improved home heating (*Account of the New Invented Pennsylvanian Fire-Places*). In July 1747, when a French fleet invaded Delaware Bay, his pamphlet, *Plain Truth,* led to a volunteer association for homeland security. Step by step, he ascended to leadership as city councilman, assemblyman, and alderman. His mother wrote, "I am glad to hear that you are so well respected in your toun for them to chuse you alderman alltho I dont know what it means nor what the better you will be of it beside the honor of it."[1] When the legislature voted Franklin to be Speaker, Pennsylvania's proprietor, Thomas Penn, called him "dangerous" as "a Sort of Tribune of the people."[2]

At the same time, Franklin devoted considerable research and writing to promoting modern popular education in *Education of Youth in Pensilvania* (1749) and *Idea of the English School* (1751). He wrote influential essays on population ("The Increase of Mankind," 1751) and on public health and hospitals. His reputation spread across the colonies for writing a proposal for a federated union at the Albany Congress (1754) and across the western world for reports on discovering the sameness of lightning and electricity, discoveries that brought honorary degrees from Harvard and Yale (1753) and the prestigious Copley Medal of Britain's Royal Society (1753). That he could devote little time to writing humorous pieces for his almanac or newspaper is less surprising than that he could write any at all.

The *Poor Richard's* prefaces, which at first served primarily to mock almanac competitors as astrologers, came to attack astrology as pseudoscience. The preface of 1751 ironically laments the deterioration of astrology—"Scarce any other Use is made of our learned Labours, than to find the best Time of cutting Corns, or gelding Pigs." Franklin's focus broadened to abuse of science generally. He decried, for instance, William Whiston's pseudoscientific signs that people were using to predict "a new Heaven and a new Earth."

By 1757, Franklin used *Poor Richard* to mock a growing class of amateurs called virtuosi. They were intrigued as much as Franklin by scientific experiments, but their ingenuity broke the bounds of common sense. Impersonating an ingenious projector and parodying the virtuosi's style, Franklin submits a useful plan for improving modern life, "How to make a Striking Sundial, by which not only a Man's own Family, but all his Neighbors for ten Miles round, may know what a Clock it is, when the Sun shines, without seeing the Dial."

Chuse an open Place in your Yard or Garden, on which the Sun may shine all Day without any Impediment from Trees or Buildings. On the Ground mark out your Hour Lines, as for a horizontal Dial, according to Art, taking Room enough for the Gun. On the Line for One o' Clock, place one Gun; on the two o' Clock Line two Guns, and so of the rest. The Guns must all be charged with Powder, but Ball is unnecessary. Your Gnomen or Style must have twelve burning Glasses annex'd to it, and be so placed as that the Sun shining through the Glasses, one after the other, shall cause the Focus or burning Spot to fall on the Hour

Line of One, for Example, at one a Clock, and there kindle a Train of Gunpowder that shall fire one Gun. At Two a Clock, a Focus shall fall on the Hour Line of Two, and kindle another Train that shall discharge two Guns successively; and so of the rest.

Note, There must be 78 Guns in all. Thirty-two Pounders will be best for this Use; but 18 Pounders may do, and will cost less, as well as use less Powder, for nine Pounds of Powder will do for one Charge of each eighteen Pounder, whereas the Thirty-two Pounders would require for each Gun 16 Pounds.

Note also, That the chief Expence will be the Powder, for the Cannon once bought, will, with Care, last 100 Years.

Note moreover, That there will be a great Saving of Powder in cloudy Days.

So far, so funny. Franklin often used this voice in newspaper pieces, relying on readers to grasp the irony. But here, mindful that almanacs had less sophisticated readers, he expounded his point.

Kind Reader, Methinks I hear thee say, *That is indeed a good Thing to know how the Time passes, but this Kind of Dial, notwithstanding the mentioned Savings, would be very expensive; and the Cost greater than the Advantage.* Thou art wise, my Friend, to be so considerate beforehand; some Fools would not have found out so much, till they had made the Dial and try'd it.—Let all such learn that many a publick Project are like this *Striking Dial,* great Cost for little Profit. [*PRA* 1757]

The comical material that appeared in the almanac or newspaper or that circulated by word of mouth seems to have been stockpiled earlier, as in the case with Poor Richard's analogy in celebrating Copernicus's birthday, January 1748.

How much more natural is *Copernicus's* Scheme! *Ptolemy* is compar'd to a whimsical Cook, who, instead of Turning the Meat in Roasting, should fix That, and contrive to have his whole Fire, Kitchen and all, whirling continually around it.

Franklin's comical pieces for the press were, of course, as timely as the passing scene at which he had a central seat. In the early 1740s, he reported a sensational story as it unfolded in the newspapers. He even composed a version in verse, and a letter undoubtedly read at the Junto, whence it circulated in copies underground down to our own time.

Last Sunday a young Fellow about 20 Years of Age was brought to Town from Whitemarsh and committed to Prison, being charg'd with Ravishing a poor old Woman upwards of Eighty, and injuring her so that her Life is tho't to be in Danger. [*Gazette,* 25 August 1743]

An Apology for the young Man in Goal, and in Shackles, for ravishing an old Woman of 85 at Whitemarsh, who had only one Eye, and that a red one.

Unhappy Youth, that could not longer stay
Till by old Age thy Choice had dy'd away;
A few Days more had given to thy Arms,
Free from the Laws, her aged Lump of Charms,
Which, tho' defunct, might feel not less alive
Than we imagine Maids of Eighty-five.
[*Mercury,* 15 September][3]

Yesterday William Coulter, a likely young Fellow of about 22 Years of Age, was tried at a Court of Oyer and Terminer, on an Indictment for ravishing a miserable old Dutch Woman of fourscore. The Jury acquitted him of the Rape, but found him guilty of an Assault. [*Gazette,* 29 September]

We hear that the old Dutch Woman, that prosecuted the young Fellow for a Rape, some time since, is lately married. [*Gazette,* 18 December 1744]

My dear Friend,

I know of no Medicine fit to diminish the violent natural Inclinations you mention; and if I did, I think I should not communicate it to you. Marriage is the proper Remedy. It is the most natural State of Man, and therefore the State in which you are most likely to find solid Happiness. Your Reasons against entring into it at present, appear to me not well-founded. The circumstantial Advantages you have in View by postponing it, are not only uncertain, but they are small in comparison with that of the Thing itself, the being *married and settled.* It is the Man and Woman united that make the compleat human being. Separate, she wants his Force of Body and Strength of Reason; he, her Softness, Sensibility and acute Discernment. Together they are more likely to succeed in the World. A single Man has not nearly the Value he would have in that State of Union. He is an incomplete Animal. He resembles the odd Half of a Pair of Scissars. If you get a prudent healthy Wife, your Industry in your Profession, with her good Œconomy, will be a Fortune sufficient.

But if you will not take this Counsel, and persist in thinking a Commerce with the Sex inevitable, then I repeat my former Advice, that in all your Amours you should *prefer old Women to young ones.* You call this a Paradox, and demand my Reasons. They are these:

1. Because as they have more Knowledge of the World and their Minds are better stor'd with Observations, their Conversation is more improving and more lastingly agreable.

2. Because when Women cease to be handsome, they study to be good. To maintain their Influence over Men, they supply the Diminution of Beauty by an Augmentation of Utility. They learn to do a 1000 Services small and great, and are the most tender and useful of all Friends when you are sick. Thus they continue amiable. And hence there is hardly such a thing to be found as an old Woman who is not a good Woman.

3. Because there is no hazard of Children, which irregularly produc'd may be attended with much Inconvenience.

4. Because thro' more Experience, they are more prudent and

discreet in conducting an Intrigue to prevent Suspicion. The Commerce with them is therefore safer with regard to your Reputation. And with regard to theirs, if the Affair should happen to be known, considerate People might be rather inclin'd to excuse an old Woman who would kindly take care of a young Man, form his Manners by her good Counsels, and prevent his ruining his Health and Fortune among mercenary prostitutes.

5. Because in every Animal that walks upright, the Deficiency of the Fluids that fill the Muscles appears first in the highest Part: The Face first grows lank and wrinkled; then the Neck; then the Breast and Arms; the lower Parts continuing to the last as plump as ever: So that covering all above with a Basket, and regarding only what is below the Girdle, it is impossible of two Women to know an old from a young one. And as in the dark all Cats are grey, the Pleasure of corporal Enjoyment with an old Woman is at least equal, and frequently superior, every Knack being by Practice capable of Improvement.

6. Because the Sin is less. The debauching a Virgin may be her Ruin, and make her for Life unhappy.

7. Because the Compunction is less. The having made a young Girl *miserable* may give you frequent bitter Reflections; none of which can attend the making an old Woman *happy.*

8. They are *so grateful!!*[4] [*Circulated in manuscript,* 25 June 1745[5]]

In the *Pennsylvania Gazette* he tried to sustain irony the way Jonathan Swift did in his modest proposal to solve famine by raising Irish children for meat. In the issue for 9 May 1751, impersonating economist Americanus, Franklin satirizes the British excuse for rejecting laws against transporting convicts to America because "Such Laws . . . tend to prevent the Improvement and Well Peopling of the Colonies." Franklin underscores the irony with italics to show the law's absurdity.

Such a tender *parental* Concern in our *Mother Country* for the Welfare of her Children, calls aloud for the highest *Returns of Gratitude and Duty.* This every one must be sensible of: But 'tis said, that in our present Circumstances it is absolutely impossible for us to make such as are adequate to the Favour. I own it; but nevertheless let us do our Endeavour. 'Tis something to show a grateful Disposition.

In some of the uninhabited Parts of these Provinces, there are Numbers of these venomous Reptiles we call **Rattle-Snakes**; Felons-convict from the Beginning of the World; These, whenever we meet with them, we put to Death, by virtue of an old Law, *Thou shalt bruise his Head.* But as this is a sanguinary Law, and may seem too cruel; and as however mischievous those Creatures are with us, they may possibly change their Natures, if they were to change the Climate; I would humbly propose, that this general Sentence of *Death* be changed for *Transportation.*

In the Spring of the Year, when they first creep out of their Holes, they are feeble, heavy, slow, and easily taken; and if a small Bounty were allow'd per Head, some Thousands might be collected annually, and *transported* to Britain. There I would propose to have them carefully distributed in *St. James's Park,* in the *Spring-Gardens* and other Places of Pleasure about *London;* in the Gardens of all the Nobility and Gentry throughout the Nation; but particularly in the Gardens of the *Prime Ministers,* the *Lords of Trade* and *Members of Parliament;* for to them we are *most particularly* obliged.

There is no human Scheme so perfect, but some Inconveniencies may be objected to it: Yet when the Conveniencies far exceed, the Scheme is judg'd rational, and fit to be executed. Thus Inconveniencies have been objected to that *good* and *wise* Act of Parliament, by virtue of which all the *Newgates* and *Dungeons* in *Britain* are emptied into the Colonies. It has been said, that these Thieves and Villains introduc'd among us, spoil the Morals of Youth in the Neighbourhoods that entertain them, and perpetrate many horrid Crimes; but let not *private Interests* obstruct *publick Utility. Our Mother* knows what is best for us. What is a little *Housebreaking, Shoplifting,* or *Highway Robbing;* what is a *Son* now and then *corrupted* and *hang'd,* a Daughter *debauch'd* and *pox'd,* a Wife *stabb'd,* a Husband's *Throat cut,* or a Child's *Brains beat out* with an Axe, compar'd with this "**Improvement and Well Peopling** of the Colonies!"

Thus it may perhaps be objected to my Scheme, that the *Rattle-Snake* is a mischievous Creature, and that his changing his Nature with the Clime is a mere Supposition, not yet confirm'd by sufficient Facts. What then? Is not Example more prevalent than Precept? And may not the honest rough British Gentry, by a Familiarity with these Reptiles, learn to *creep,* and to *insinuate,* and to *slaver,* and to *wriggle* into Place (and perhaps to *poison* such as stand in their Way) Qualities of no small Advantage to Courtiers! In comparison of which "*Improvement* and *Publick Utility,*" what is a *Child* now and then kill'd by their venomous Bite, —or even a favourite *Lap-Dog?*

I would only add, That this Exporting of Felons to the Colonies, may be consider'd as a *Trade,* as well as in the Light of a Favour. Now all Commerce implies *Returns:* Justice requires them: There can be no Trade without them. And *Rattle-Snakes* seem the most *suitable Returns* for the *Human Serpents* sent us by our *Mother* Country. In this, however, as in every other Branch of Trade, she will have the Advantage of us. She will reap *equal* Benefits without equal Risque of the Inconveniencies and Dangers. For the *Rattle-Snake* gives Warning before he attempts his Mischief; which the Convict does not. [*Pennsylvania Gazette,* 9 May 1751]

Another piece likely prepared to be read for the Junto appeared first in the London *General Advertiser* (15 April 1747), then London's *Gentleman's Magazine.* After being reprinted repeatedly abroad, the speech was published in Jonas Greene's *Maryland Gazette* in a more complete version as if directly from Franklin himself. His "Speech of Miss Polly Baker" sustained its comic stance so well as to fool historians that she had been an actual single parent harassed by her Puritan contemporaries. During Franklin's visit to New England in winter 1746, he could have heard of a prototype in Eleonor Kellog of Worcester. The previous year, she had been fined and whipped for fornication and child-bearing, "a 5th Crime."[6] Franklin artfully fused this and literary models with comical touches of his own.[7] The humorous title in the *Maryland Gazette* (11 August 1747) has her wed one of the judges. Her plea, parodying a classical oration,[8] concludes with a salacious pun on the last words of Swift's "Modest Proposal." Franklin's impersonation of this fiercely independent woman has endeared her to modern readers sensitive to the problems of single mothers. In thus celebrating the lust for life, she stands thigh to thigh with Chaucer's Wife of Bath. Franklin's comic spirit reconciles the fallibility of human nature with the laws of man, nature, and nature's God.

The ***Speech*** *of Miss Polly Baker, before a Court of Judicature, at Connecticut in New England, where she was prosecuted the fifth Time for having a Bastard Child; which influenced the Court to dispense with her Punishment, and induced one of her Judges to marry her the next Day.*

May it please the Honourable Bench to indulge me a few Words: I am a poor unhappy Woman; who have no Money to Fee Lawyers to plead for me, being hard put to it to get a tolerable Living. I shall not trouble your Honours with long Speeches; for I have not the presumption to expect, that you may, by any Means, be prevailed on to deviate in your Sentence from the Law, in my Favour. All I humbly hope is, that your Honours would charitably move the Governor's Goodness on my Behalf, that my Fine may be remitted. This is the Fifth Time, gentlemen, that I have been dragg'd before your Courts on the same Account; twice I have paid heavy Fines, and twice have been brought to public Punishment, for want of Money to pay those Fines. This may have been agreeable to the Laws; I do not dispute it: But since Laws are sometimes unreasonable in themselves, and therefore repealed; and others bear too hard on the Subject in particular Circumstances; and therefore there is left a Power somewhere to dispense with the Execution of them; I take the Liberty to say, that I think this Law, by which I am punished, is both unreasonable in itself, and particularly severe with regard to me, who have always lived an inoffensive Life in the Neighbourhood where I was born, and defy my Enemies (if I have any) to say I ever wrong'd Man, Woman or Child. Abstracted from the Law, I cannot conceive (may it please your Honours) what the Nature of my Offence is. I have brought Five fine Children into the World, at the Risque of my Life: I have maintained them well by my own Industry, without burthening the Township, and could have done it better, if it had not been for the heavy Charges and Fines I have paid. Can it be a Crime (in the Nature of Things I mean) to add to the Number of the King's Subjects, in a new Country that really wants People? I own I should think it rather a Praise worthy, than a Punishable Action. I have debauch'd no other Woman's Husband, nor inticed any innocent Youth: These Things I never was charged with; nor has any one the least cause of Complaint against me, unless, perhaps the Minister, or the Justice, because I have had Children without being Married, by which they have miss'd a Wedding Fee. But, can even this be a Fault of mine? I appeal to your Honours. You are pleased to allow I don't want Sense; but I must be stupid to the last Degree, not to prefer the honourable State of Wedlock, to the Condition I have lived in. I always was, and still am, willing to enter into it; I doubt not my Behaving well in it, having all the Industry, Frugality, Fertility, and Skill in Œconomy, appertaining to a good Wife's Character. I defy any Person to say I ever Refused an Offer of that Sort: On the contrary, I readily Consented to the only Proposal of Marriage that ever was made me, which was when I was a Virgin; but too easily confiding in the Person's Sincerity that made it, I unhappily lost my own Honour, by trusting to his; for he got me with Child, and then forsook me: That very Person you all know; he is now become a Magistrate of this County; and I had hopes he would have appeared this Day on the Bench, and have endeavoured to moderate the Court in my Favour; then I should have scorn'd to have mention'd it; but I must Complain of it as unjust and unequal, that my Betrayer and Undoer, the first Cause of all my Faults and Miscarriages (if they must be deemed such) should be advanced to Honour and Power, in the same

Government that punishes my Misfortunes with Stripes and Infamy. I shall be told, 'tis like, that were there no Act of Assembly in the Case, the Precepts of Religion are violated by my Transgressions. If mine, then, is a religious Offence, leave it, Gentlemen, to religious Punishments. You have already excluded me from all the Comforts of your Church Communion: Is not that sufficient? You believe I have offended Heaven, and must suffer eternal Fire: Will not that be sufficient? What need is there, then, of your additional Fines and Whippings? I own, I do not think as you do; for, if I thought, what you call Sin, was really such, I would not presumptuously commit it. But how can it be believed, that Heaven is angry at my having Children, when, to the little done by me towards it, God has been pleased to add his divine Skill and admirable Workmanship in the Formation of their Bodies, and crown'd it by furnishing them with rational and immortal Souls? Forgive me Gentlemen, if I talk a little extravagantly on these Matters; I am no Divine: But if you, great Men, [*Turning to some Gentlemen of the Assembly, then in Court*] must be making Laws, do not turn natural and useful Actions into Crimes, by your Prohibitions. Reflect a little on the horrible Consequences of this Law in particular: What Numbers of procur'd Abortions! and how many distress'd Mothers have been driven, by the Terror of Punishment and public Shame, to imbrue, contrary to Nature, their own trembling Hands in the Blood of their helpless Offspring! Nature would have induc'd them to nurse it up with a Parent's Fondness. 'Tis the Law therefore, 'tis the Law itself that is guilty of all these Barbarities and Murders. Repeal it then, Gentlemen; let it be expung'd for ever from your Books: And on the other hand, take into your wise Consideration, the great and growing Number of Batchelors in the Country, many of whom, from the mean Fear of the Expence of a Family, have never sincerely and honourably Courted a Woman in their Lives; and by their Manner of Living, leave unproduced (which I think is little better than Murder) Hundreds of their Posterity to the Thousandth Generation. Is not theirs a greater Offence against the Public Good, than mine? Compel them then, by a Law, either to Marry, or pay double the Fine of Fornication every Year. What must poor young Women do, whom Custom has forbid to solicit the Men, and who cannot force themselves upon Husbands, when the Laws take no Care to provide them any, and yet severely punish if they do their Duty without them? Yes, Gentlemen, I venture to call it a Duty; 'tis the Duty of the first and great Command of Nature, and of Nature's God, *Increase and multiply:* a Duty, from the steady Performance of which nothing has ever been able to deter me; but for it's Sake, I have hazarded the Loss of the public Esteem, and frequently incurr'd public Disgrace and Punishment; and therefore ought, in my humble Opinion, instead of a Whipping, to have a Statue erected to my Memory. [*Maryland Gazette,* 11 August 1747]

It would take another ten years for Franklin to find leisure enough to recapture the comic art of Polly Baker. After he was appointed Pennsylvania's agent to London, he had to endure three months of enforced idleness while awaiting permission to sail from the British official Lord Loudon—as notorious for compulsive writing as Father Abraham was for speaking. In Poor Richard's final preface for 1758, Franklin expanded the customary one-page preface to fifteen, printing portions of Father Abraham's sermon on every calendar page. He limited Poor Richard's lines to three introductory paragraphs plus one in conclusion.

Franklin's preface, reprinted in Boston as a commercial venture by his nephew Benny Mecom and subsequently overseas as "The Way to Wealth," would be translated into many languages and distributed around the world, and become one of the most popular publications in nineteenth-century America. But by deleting its introductory paragraphs, the later reprints diluted Franklin's satire of Poor Richard himself.

Even more than Polly Baker's speech, "The Way to Wealth" was so crafted as to fool generations of readers unaware that they too were among Franklin's targets: (1) Father Abraham as sidewalk Polonius, (2) Poor Richard gulled by his own words, and (3) readers carried away by the immediacy of the narrative and dialogue to overlook the difference. Distracted by Father

Abraham's mix of banal clichés and old-fashioned common sense, we sometimes overlook that Poor Richard stands out in the crowd as the only one who practices what the old man preaches. This oversight results from Franklin's distancing himself from Poor Richard's point of view, a device he used in having Silence Dogood tell how on her evening walk she eavesdropped on conversation about herself. Poor Richard listens in an even more dramatic mode.

Courteous Reader,

I have heard that nothing gives an Author so great Pleasure, as to find his Works respectfully quoted by other learned Authors. This Pleasure I have seldom enjoyed; for tho' I have been, if I may say it without Vanity, an *eminent Author* of Almanacks annually now a full Quarter of a Century, my Brother Authors in the same Way, for what Reason I know not, have ever been very sparing in their Applauses; and no other Author has taken the least Notice of me, so that did not my Writings produce me some solid *Pudding,* the great Deficiency of *Praise* would have quite discouraged me.

I concluded at length, that the People were the best Judges of my Merit; for they buy my Works; and besides, in my Rambles, where I am not personally known, I have frequently heard one or other of my Adages repeated, with, *as Poor Richard says,* at the End on't; this gave me some Satisfaction, as it showed not only that my Instructions were regarded, but discovered likewise some Respect for my Authority; and I own, that to encourage the Practice of remembering and repeating those wise Sentences, I have sometimes *quoted myself* with great Gravity.

Judge then how much I must have been gratified by an Incident I am going to relate to you. I stopt my Horse lately where a great Number of People were collected at a Vendue of Merchant Goods. The Hour of Sale not being come, they were conversing on the Badness of the Times, and one of the Company call'd to a plain clean old Man, with white Locks, *Pray, Father* Abraham, *what think you of the Times? Won't these heavy Taxes quite ruin the Coun-*

try? How shall we be ever able to pay them? What would you advise us to?—

> The focus on taxes reflects Franklin's current political conflict with proprietor Thomas Penn, who resisted the Pennsylvania legislature's pleas to pay a fair share of taxes for defense in the French and Indian War.

Father Abraham stood up, and reply'd, If you'd have my Advice, I'll give it you in short, for a *Word to the Wise is enough,* and *many Words won't fill a Bushel, as Poor Richard says.* They join'd in desiring him to speak his Mind, and gathering round him, he proceeded as follows;

Friends, says he, and Neighbours, the Taxes are indeed very heavy, and if those laid on by the Government were the only Ones we had to pay, we might more easily discharge them; but we have many others, and much more grievous to some of us. We are taxed twice as much by our *Idleness,* three times as much by our *Pride,* and four times as much by our *Folly,* and from these Taxes the Commissioners cannot ease or deliver us by allowing an Abatement. However let us hearken to good Advice, and something may be done for us; *God helps them that help themselves,* as Poor Richard says, in his Almanac of 1733.

> Father Abraham misremembers the date (1736) as he turns from promoting industry to preaching perseverance and prudence in everyday life. [9]

It would be thought a hard Government that should tax its People one tenth Part of their *Time,* to be employed in its Service. But *Idleness* taxes many of us much more, if we reckon all that is spent in absolute *Sloth* . . . [that], by bringing on Diseases, absolutely shortens Life. *Sloth, like Rust, consumes faster than Labour wears, while the used Key is always bright,* as *Poor Richard,* says. But *dost thou love Life, then do not squander Time, for that's the Stuff Life is made of,* as *Poor Richard* says.—

How much more than is necessary do we spend in Sleep! forgetting that *The sleeping Fox catches no Poultry,* and that *there will be sleeping enough in the Grave,* as *Poor Richard* says. If Time be of all Things the most precious, *wasting Time* must be, as *Poor Richard* says, *the greatest prodigality,* since, as he elsewhere tells us, *Lost Time is never found again;* and what we call *Time-enough, always proves little enough:* Let us then up and be doing, and doing to the Purpose; so by Diligence shall we do more with less Perplexity. *Sloth makes all Things difficult, but Industry all easy,* as *Poor Richard* says; and *He that riseth late, must trot all Day, and shall scarce overtake his Business at Night.* While *Laziness travels so slowly, that Poverty soon overtakes him,* as we read in *Poor Richard,* who adds, *Drive thy Business, let not that drive thee;* and *Early to Bed, and early to rise, makes a Man healthy, wealthy and wise. . . .*

What though you have found no Treasure, nor has any rich Relation left you a Legacy, *Diligence is the Mother of Good-luck,* as *Poor Richard* says, *and God gives all Things to Industry.* Then *plough deep while Sluggards sleep, and you shall have Corn to sell and to keep,* says, Poor Dick. Work while it is called To-day, for you know not how much you may be hindered To-morrow, which makes *Poor Richard* say, *One To-day is worth two Tomorrows;* and farther, *Have you somewhat to do To-morrow, do it To-day.* If you were a Servant, would you not be ashamed that a good Master should catch you idle? Are you then your own Master, *be ashamed to catch yourself idle,* as *Poor Dick* says. When there is so much to be done for yourself, your Family, your Country, and your gracious King, be up by Peep of Day; *Let not the Sun look down and say, Inglorious here he lies.* Handle your Tools without Mittens; remember that *the Cat in Gloves catches no Mice,* as *Poor Richard* says. 'Tis true there is much to be done, and perhaps you are weak handed, but stick to it steadily, and you will see great Effects, for *constant Dropping wears away Stones,* and by *Diligence and Patience the Mouse ate in two the Cable;* and *little Strokes fell great Oaks,* as *Poor Richard* says in his Almanack, the Year I cannot just now remember.

Methinks I hear some of you say, *Must a Man afford himself no Leisure?*—I will tell thee, my Friend, what *Poor Richard* says, *Em-*

ploy thy Time well if thou meanest to gain Leisure; and, *since thou art not sure of a Minute, throw not away an Hour.* Leisure, is Time for doing something useful; this Leisure the diligent Man will obtain, but the lazy Man never; so that, as *Poor Richard* says, a *Life of Leisure and a Life of Laziness are two Things. . . . Many without Labour, would live by their* **Wits** *only, but they break for Want of Stock.* Whereas Industry gives Comfort, and Plenty, and Respect: *Fly Pleasures, and they'll follow you. The diligent Spinner has a large Shift;* and *now I have Sheep and a Cow, every Body bids me Good morrow. . . .*

But with our Industry, we must likewise be *steady, settled* and *careful,* and oversee our own Affairs *with our own Eyes,* and not trust too much to others; for as *Poor Richard* says,

I never saw an oft removed Tree,
Nor yet an oft removed Family,
That throve so well as those that settled be.

And again, *Three Removes is as bad as a Fire;* and again, *Keep thy Shop, and thy Shop will keep thee;* and again, *If you would have your Business done, go; if not, send.* And again,

He that by the Plough would thrive,
Himself must either hold or drive. . . .

And again, he adviseth to Circumspection and Care, even in the smallest Matters, because sometimes *a little Neglect may breed great Mischief;* adding, *For want of a Nail the Shoe was lost; for want of a Shoe the Horse was lost; and for want of a Horse the Rider was lost,* being overtaken and slain by the Enemy, all for want of Care about a Horse-shoe Nail.

Father Abraham turns from preaching to the people at the auction to exhorting readers generally. The idea of practicing austerity to bolster national economy, whether meant to be taken seriously or not, would soon become colonial policy in the movement to secure independence from London merchants and ultimately from Great Britain.

So much for Industry, my Friends, and Attention to one's own Business; but to these we must add *Frugality,* if we would make our Industry more certainly successful. A Man may, if he knows not how to save as he gets, *keep his Nose all his Life to the Grindstone,* and die not worth a Groat at last. *A fat Kitchen makes a lean Will,* as Poor Richard says; and

Many Estates are spent in the Getting,
Since Women for Tea forsook Spinning and Knitting,
And Men for Punch forsook Hewing and Splitting. . . .
Women and Wine, Game and Deceit,
Make the Wealth small, and the Wants great.

And farther, *What maintains one Vice, would bring up two Children.* You may think perhaps, That a *little* Tea, or a *little* Punch now and then, Diet a *little* more costly, Clothes a *little* finer, and a *little* Entertainment now and then, can be no *great* Matter; but remember what *Poor Richard* says, *Many* a Little *makes a Mickle;* and farther, *Beware of* little *Expences; a small leak will sink a great Ship;* and again, *Who Dainties love, shall Beggars prove;* and moreover, *Fools make Feasts, and wise Men eat them.*

Here you are all got together at this Vendue of *Fineries* and *Knicknacks.* You call them *Goods,* but if you do not take Care, they will prove *Evils* to some of you. You expect they will be sold *cheap,* and perhaps they may for less than they cost; but if you have no Occasion for them, they must be *dear* to you. Remember what *Poor Richard* says, *Buy what thou hast no Need of, and ere long thou shalt sell they Necessaries.* And again, *At a great Pennyworth pause a while:* He means, that perhaps the Cheapness is *apparent* only, and not *real. . . .*

Again, *Poor Richard* says, *'Tis foolish to lay out Money in a Purchase of Repentance;* and yet this Folly is practised every Day at Vendues, for want of minding the Almanack. . . . Many a one, for the Sake of Finery on the Back, have gone with a hungry Belly, and half starved their Families; *Silks and Sattins, Scarlet and Velvets,* as *Poor Richard* says, *put out the Kitchen Fire.* These are not the *Necessaries* of Life; they can scarcely be called the *Conveniencies,* and yet only because they look pretty, how many *want* to *have* them. The *artificial* Wants of Mankind thus become more numerous than the *natural.* . . . The Genteel are reduced to Poverty, and forced to borrow of those whom they formerly despised, but who through *Industry* and *Frugality* have maintained their Standing; in which case it appears plainly, that a *Ploughman on his Legs is higher than a Gentleman on his Knees.* . . . As *Poor Dick* says, . . . *If you would know the Value of Money, go and try to borrow some;* for, *he that goes a borrowing goes a sorrowing;* and indeed so does he that lends to such people, when he goes *to get it in again.*—

Finally, Father Abraham proposes prudence as the means of prevailing against London merchants, bankers, and military officials such as Lord Loudon, who was then delaying Franklin's passage to London, and political authorities such as proprietor Thomas Penn, whose power he was sailing to London to challenge.

Poor Dick farther advises, and says,
Fond Pride of Dress, *is sure a very Curse;*
E'er Fancy *you consult, consult your Purse.* . . .

'Tis as truly Folly for the Poor to ape the Rich, as for the Frog to swell, in order to equal the Ox.

Great Estates may venture more,
But little Boats should keep near Shore.

'Tis however a Folly soon punished; for *Pride that dines on Vanity sups on Contempt,* as *Poor Richard* says. . . . What Madness must it be to *run in Debt* for these Superfluities! We are offered, by the Terms of this Vendue, *Six months Credit;* and that perhaps has induced some of us to attend it, because we cannot spare the ready Money, and hope now to be fine without it. But, ah, think what you do when you run in Debt; *You give to another Power over your Liberty.* If you cannot pay at the Time, you will be ashamed to see your Creditor; you will be in Fear when you speak to him; you will make poor pitiful sneaking Excuses, and by degrees come to lose your Veracity, and, sink into base downright lying; for, as *Poor Richard* says, *The second Vice is Lying, the first is running into Debt.* And again, to the same Purpose, *Lying rides upon Debt's Back.* Whereas a freeborn *Englishman* ought not to be ashamed or afraid to see or speak to any Man living. But Poverty often deprives a Man of all Spirit and Virtue; *'Tis hard for an empty Bag to stand upright.* . . . Then since, as he says, *The Borrower is a Slave to the Lender, and the Debtor to the Creditor,* disdain the Chain, preserve your Freedom; and maintain your Independency: Be *industrious* and *free; be* frugal *and* free. . . .

Get what you can, and what you get hold;
'Tis the Stone that will turn all your Lead into Gold,

as *Poor Richard* says. And when you have got the Philosopher's Stone, sure you will no longer complain of bad Times, or the Difficulty of paying Taxes.

This Doctrine, my Friends, is *Reason* and *Wisdom;* but after all, do not depend too much upon your own *Industry,* and *Frugality,* and *Prudence,* though excellent Things, for they may all be blasted without the Blessing of Heaven. . . . And now to conclude, *Experience keeps a dear School, but Fools will learn in no other, and scarce in that;* for it is true, *we may give Advice, but we cannot give Conduct,* as *Poor Richard* says: However, remember this, *They that won't be counselled, can't be helped,* as *Poor Richard* says: And farther, *If you will not hear Reason, she'll surely rap your Knuckles.*

Thus the old Gentleman ended his Harangue. The People heard it, and approved the Doctrine, and immediately practised the contrary, just as if it had been a common Sermon; for the Vendue opened, and they began to buy extravagantly, notwithstanding all his Cautions, and their own Fear of Taxes.—

I found the good Man had thoroughly studied my Almanacks, and digested all I had dropt on those Topicks during the Course of Five-and-twenty Years. The frequent Mention he made of me must have tired any one else, but my Vanity was wonderfully delighted with it, though I was conscious that not a tenth Part of the Wisdom was my own which he ascribed to me, but rather the *Gleanings* I had made of the Sense of all Ages and Nations. However, I resolved to be the better for the Echo of it; and though I had at first determined to buy Stuff for a new Coat, I went away resolved to wear my old One a little longer. *Reader,* if thou wilt do the same, thy Profit will be as great as mine. *[Poor Richard Improved,* 1758]

In thus satirizing the human frailty of Father Abraham, Richard Saunders, and his readers, Franklin could have included himself as victim of unintended consequences in that critics in the twentieth century like D. H. Lawrence blamed him for the gospel of materialism. But Father Abraham's speech, along with that of Polly Baker, showed increasing independence from such earlier models as the *Spectator.* Besides fusing empirical and literary models, he now cultivated his earlier publications as seedbed of an indigenous comic spirit.

5

MAKING FRIENDS OVERSEAS

1757–1774

As Pennsylvania's agent in London, Franklin had to wait three years for the courts to make proprietor Thomas Penn pay his fair share for provincial defense. Franklin used that time and two more years enjoying club life, honors, and new friends among leaders of the liberal religious, intellectual, cultural, and political communities, enlarging the circle with visits to France, Germany, Ireland, and Scotland. The universities of Saint Andrews and Oxford granted him honorary doctorates. He attended the coronation of George III. Conviviality, congeniality, and ceremony left little time for composing anything other than official or technical reports. Accustomed to using humor for attack or defense in business and politics, he found it also useful in relieving pressures of public service by writing "familiar letters."

James Howell's *Epistolae Ho-Elianae* (1645–1655) had popularized composing familiar letters as written conversation—"We should write as we speak," said Howell.[1] The pen, he said, should impersonate the mind in motion as it processes news, jokes, anecdotes, and impromptu aphorisms, such as "One foot cannot be up till the other be down." The allusions that bubble up in the process and the language too should be adjusted to the readers whose assumptions and attitudes the writer shares and also to the role assumed by the writer. Franklin had already developed this style in impersonating characters such as Silence Dogood and Poor Richard. He now followed fashion by impersonating his own mind in motion, as when writing to his only surviving sister, Jane Mecom, about the vanity of dogmatizing. He recollects verses from Howells (misremembered as "an Ancient Poet") merely to show that every doggerel hath its day.

You may remember an Ancient Poet whose Words we have all Studied and Copy'd at School, said long ago,

A Man of Words and not of Deeds.
Is like a Garden full of Weeds.

'Tis pity that *Good Works* among some sorts of People are so little Valued, and *Good Words* admired in their Stead; I mean seemingly *pious Discourses* instead of *Humane Benevolent Actions*. . . . When you mention *Virtue*, they pucker up their Noses as if they smelt a Stink; at the same time that they eagerly snuff up an empty canting Harangue, as if it was a Posie of the Choicest Flowers. So they have inverted the good old Verse, and say now

A Man of Deeds and not of Words
Is like a Garden full of——

I have forgot the Rhime, but remember 'tis something the very Reverse of a Perfume.[2]

As in conversation, Franklin would of course adjust to his company. In the spirit of fun, he teases his landlady's twenty-one-year-old daughter, Polly Stevenson, for fuzzy thinking while he himself misremembers an anecdote from John Selden's *Table Talk* (1689) about Lady Cotten interrupting her husband as he speculates on whether an old shoe once belonged to Moses or to Noah.[3]

This Prudence of not attempting to give Reasons before one is sure of Facts, I learnt from one of your Sex, who, as Selden tells us, being in company with some Gentlemen that were viewing and considering something they call'd a Chinese Shoe, and disputing earnestly about the manner of wearing it, and how it could possibly be put on; put in her Word, and said modestly, *Gentlemen, are you sure it is a Shoe?*[4]

In writing to a more sophisticated acquaintance, Birmingham typographer John Baskerville, Franklin alludes to technical details to ridicule a pretentious critic of Baskerville's new typeface and puns on the double meaning of *character* as respecting persons or printers' type.

Let me give you a pleasant Instance of the Prejudice some have entertained against your Work. Soon after I returned, discoursing with a gentleman concerning the Artists of Birmingham, he said you would be a means of Blinding all the Readers in the Nation, for the Strokes of your Letters being too thin and narrow, hurt the Eye, and he could never read a Line of them without Pain.

I thought, said I, you were going to complain of the Gloss on the paper, some object to; No, no, says he, I have heard that mentioned, but it is not that; 'tis in the Form and Cut of the Letters themselves; they have not that natural and easy Proportion between the Height and Thickness of the Stroke, which makes the common printing so much more comfortable to the Eye. You see this Gentleman was a Connoisseur. In vain I endeavoured to support your *Character* against the Charge; he knew what he felt, he could see the Reason of it, and several other gentlemen among his Friends had made the same Observation, &c.

Yesterday he called to visit me, when, mischievously bent to try his judgment, I stept into my Closet, tore off the Top of Mr. Caslon's Specimen, and produc'd it to him as yours brought with me from Birmingham, saying, I had been examining it since he spoke to me, and could not for my Life perceive the Disproportion he mentioned, desiring him to point it out to me.

He readily undertook it, and went over several Founts, shewing me everywhere what he thought Instances of that Disproportion; and declared, that he could not read the Specimen without feeling very strongly the Pain he had mentioned to me. I spared him that Time the Confusion of being told, that these were the Types he had been reading all his Life with so much Ease to his Eyes; the Types his adored Newton is printed with, on which he has pored not a little; nay, the very Types his own Book is printed with, for he is himself an Author; and yet never discovered this painful Disproportion in them, till he thought they were yours.[5]

Franklin writes to a more sophisticated friend, historian-philosopher David Hume, about their mutual friend Lord Marischal being asked to resolve a villagers' dispute on eternal damnation. In good familiar letter form, Franklin alludes to an obscure historic conflict that Hume would have recognized, probably the one at Banbury, 1589, which the Privy Council was called upon to resolve and did so by decree somewhat similar to the Lord Marischal's.[6]

The Church People and the Puritans in a Country Town, had once a bitter Contention concerning the Erecting of a Maypole, which the former desir'd and the latter oppos'd. Each Party endeavour'd to strengthen itself by obtaining the Authority of the Mayor, directing or forbidding a Maypole. He heard their Altercation with great Patience, and then gravely determin'd thus; You that are for having no Maypole shall have no Maypole; and you that are for having a Maypole shall have a Maypole. Get about your Business and let me hear no more of this Quarrel. So methinks Lord Marischal might say; You that are for no more Damnation than is proportion'd to your Offences, have my Consent that it may be so: And you that are for being damn'd eternally, G-d eternally da—n you all, and let me hear no more of your Disputes.[7]

Returning to Philadelphia in November 1762, Franklin headed a party to repeal proprietary government altogether. As copostmaster for British North America, he toured the Northeast and New England and thus cemented intercolonial unity at a time when Parliament imposed taxes on sugar and restricted colonies from issuing currency. He was elected speaker of the Assembly, only to lose his seat in the bitter October 1764 election that slandered his political motives and sexual mores. His partisans reappointed him Pennsylvania's agent in London just in time to face the obnoxious Stamp Act that taxed printed paper of any kind—legal documents as well as newspapers.

Back in London, Franklin lobbied with English friends and merchants for Stamp Act repeal. In a highly publicized hearing, he warned Parliament that Americans were not in rebellion but might very well make one. Americans reacted with boycotts, mob action, and an intercolonial Congress. After being in force only a year, the Stamp Act was repealed, but the controversy smoldered on.

During the anti–Stamp Act campaign, Franklin countered anti-American propaganda in the British press with political satire. Responding to restrictions on American imports, he impersonated a far-flung world traveler in the newspaper of a friend, Sam Woodfall, the *Public Advertiser.* He parroted disinformation spewing from the London press, fusing actual passages from newspapers published during February and May 1765 with the story of long-tailed sheep from Herodotus[8] and Rabelais,[9] and an exaggeration of his own based on a report from Quebec in the *Public Advertiser* a month earlier.

Give me Leave to instance the various numberless Accounts the News-Writers have given us (with so much honest Zeal for the Welfare of Poor Old England!) of the establishing Manufactures in the Colonies to the Prejudice of those in this Kingdom. It is objected by superficial Readers, who yet pretend to some Knowledge of those Countries, that such Establishments are not only improbable but impossible; for that their Sheep have but little Wool, not in the whole sufficient for a Pair of Stockings a Year to each Inhabitant; and that, from the universal Dearness of Labour among them, the working of Iron and other Materials, except in Plowshares, Cart Wheel Tires and such bulky & coarse Things, is impracticable to any Advantage. Dear Sir, do not let us suffer ourselves to be amused with such groundless Objections. The very Tails of the American Sheep are so laden with Wool, that each has a Car or Waggon on four little Wheels to support and keep it from trailing on the Ground. . . .

This is as certainly true as the Account, said to be from Quebec, in the Papers of last Week, that the Inhabitants of Canada are making Preparations for a Cod and Whale Fishery this Summer in the Upper Lakes. Ignorant People may object that the Upper Lakes are fresh, and that Cod and Whale are Salt-water Fish; But let them know, Sir, that Cod, like other Fish, when attacked by their Enemies, fly into any Water where they think they can be safest; that Whales, when they have a Mind to eat Cod, pursue them wherever they fly; and that the grand Leap of the Whale in that Chace up the Fall of Niagara is esteemed by all who have seen it, as one of the finest Spectacles in Nature![10]

In London newspapers friendly to America—the *Daily Advertiser,* which printed at least forty of his pieces, and the *Gazetteer*[11]—Franklin maintained a flow of pseudonymous political letters winking at popular topics. Responding to critics like "Vindex," who complained about riotous New Yorkers resisting orders to billet British troops, Franklin, as "F.B.," advised Vindex to discriminate between scoundrels and the "whole people"; he concluded with a bilingual pun. Franklin's "scant knowledge" of French was sufficient to know an innkeeper's cry meant "in a minute."[12] But the apologue played with the practice of lower classes aping aristocrats by vacationing in Paris (even during a season when tailors were striking for a living wage).[13]

Two journeymen *Snips,* during the season of little business, agreed to make a trip to Paris, with each a fine lac'd waistcoat , in which they promised themselves the great pleasure of being received and treated as *gentlemen.* On the road from Calais, at every inn, when they called for any thing hastily, they were answered, *Tout a l'heure, Tout a l'heure;* which not a little surprized them. At length, D— these French scoundrels, says one, how *shrewd* they are! I find it won't do;—e'en let us go back again to London.—Aye, says t'other, they must certainly deal with the devil, or, dress'd as we are dress'd, they could not possibly all at first sight have known us to be *two taylors.*[14]

Franklin, again as "F.B." in the *Public Advertiser,* used another popular story about Londoners in Paris to ridicule government policy. Although the Stamp Act had been repealed, the cost of administering the act was estimated as 64,000 pounds (actually closer to 7,000), which Parliament expected the Americans to pay.[15]

The whole Proceeding would put one in Mind of the Frenchman that used to accost English and other Strangers on the *Pont-Neuf* (a bridge over the River Seine, leading to Paris) with many Compliments, and a red hot Iron in his Hand; *Pray Monsieur Anglois,* says he, *Do me the Favour to let me have the Honour of thrusting this hot Iron into your Backside?* Zoons, what does the Fellow mean! Begone with your Iron, or I'll break your Head! *Nay, Monsieur,* replies he, *if you do not chuse it, I do not insist upon it. But at least, you will in Justice have the Goodness to pay me something for the heating of my Iron.*[16]

Angered at Parliament's mean attitude, Franklin returned to his Swiftian mode. Ten years earlier, in the *Pennsylvania Gazette,* he had merely proposed exchanging rattlesnakes for criminals transported from England. In April 1766, with Parliament about to extend the practice of transportation to embrace Scots felons, Franklin circulated a mock petition to transport American felons to Scotland,[17] and as "Pacificus" in the *Public Advertiser* (23 January 1766), he proposed bloodthirsty measures to both pacify Americans and find a use for their new immigrants.

The Business might be done without employing any of the Regular Troops quartered in the Country, and I think it would be best they should remain neuter, as it is to be feared they would be rather backward in embruing their Hands in the Blood of their Brethren and Fellow Subjects. I would propose, that all the Capitals of the several Provinces should be burnt to the Ground, and that they cut the Throats of all the Inhabitants, Men, Women, and Children, and scalp them, to serve as an Example: that all the Shipping should be destroyed, which will effectually prevent Smuggling, and save the Expence of Guarda Costas [revenuers].

No Man in his Wits, after such terrible Military Execution, will refuse to purchase stamp'd Paper. If any one should hesitate, five or six Hundred Lashes in a cold frosty Morning would soon bring him to Reason.

If the Massacre should be objected to, as it would too much depopulate the Country, it may be replied, that the Interruption this Method would occasion to Commerce, would cause so many Bankruptcies, such Numbers of Manufacturers and Labourers would be unemployed, that, together with the Felons from our Gaols, we should soon be enabled to transport such Numbers to repeople the Colonies, as to make up for any Deficiency which Example made it Necessary to sacrifice for the Public Good. Great Britain might then reign over a loyal and submissive People, and be morally certain, that no Act of Parliament would ever after be disputed.[18]

When Franklin himself vacationed in Paris, in September and October 1767, his familiar letters reported how he enrolled himself among the ridiculous tourists. He told how, before visiting the royal court, he suffered the obligatory hair-raising experience.

I had not been here Six Days before my Taylor and Perquier had transform'd me into a Frenchman. Only think what a Figure I make in a little Bag Wig and naked Ears! They told me I was become 20 Years younger, and look'd very galante; so being in Paris where the Mode is to be sacredly follow'd, I was once very near making Love to my Friend's Wife.[19]

Another of Franklin's familiar letters burlesqued the official Court gazette. He was following the model of popular jest books that burlesqued rural newspapers with such items as "From the Squire's House—It is reported that the Minister christened a Male Child last Week, but it wants *Confirmation.*"[20] When landlady Margaret Stevenson went on vacation, daughter Polly and her new husband William Hewson, both referred to as the Ministry, moved to Craven Street to look after both the house and Franklin. For the absent Margaret Stevenson, Franklin compiled the *Craven Street Gazette,* a potpourri of domestic gossip along with a virtual battle of correspondents, with the newlyweds as antagonists and himself as put-upon protagonist. As random excerpts show, the motto of the *Craven Street Gazette* should have been, "All the News that Fits, We Print."

Saturday, 22 September 1770. We hear that the *great* Person (so called from, his enormous Size) . . . intended to pay his respects to another great Personage this Day, at St. James's, it being Coronation-Day; hoping thereby a little to amuse his Grief; but was prevented by an Accident, Queen Margaret, or her Maid of Honour having carried off the Key of the Drawers, so that the Lady of the Bedchamber could not come at a laced Shirt for his Highness. Great Clamours were made on this Occasion against her Majesty.

Sunday, 23 September. It is now found by sad Experience, that good Resolutions are easier made than executed. Notwithstanding yesterday's solemn Order of Council, no body went to Church to day. It seems the *great* Person's broad-built-bulk lay so long abed, that Breakfast was not over till it was too late to dress. At least this is the Excuse. In fine, it seems a vain thing to hope Reformation from the Example of our great Folks. . . . Dr. Fatsides made 469 Turns in his Dining Room as the exact Distance of a Visit to the lovely Lady [Mary] Barwell, whom he did not find at home, so there was no Struggle for and against a Kiss, and he sat down to dream in the Easy Chair that he had it without any Trouble.

Tuesday, 25 September. A terrible Accident had *liked to have happened* this Afternoon at Tea. The Boiler was set too near the End of the little square Table. The first Ministress was sitting at one end of the Table to administer the Tea; the great Person was about to sit down at the other End where the Boiler stood. By a sudden Motion, the Lady gave the Table a Tilt. Had it gone over, the great *Person* must have been scalded; perhaps to Death. Various are the Surmises and Observations on this Occasion. The Godly say, it would have been a just Judgment on him, for preventing by his Laziness, the Family's going to Church last Sunday. The Opposition do not stick to insinuate that there was a Design to scald him, prevented only by his quick Catching the Table. The Friends of the Ministry give out, that he carelessly jogg'd the Table himself, and would have been inevitably scalded had not the Ministress sav'd him. It is hard for the Publick to come at the Truth in these Cases.

Monday, 24 September. We are credibly informed, that the *great* Person dined this Day with the Club at the Cat-and-Bagpipes in the City, on cold Round of boil'd Beef. This, it seems, he was under some Necessity of Doing (tho' he rather dislikes Beef) because truly the Ministers were to be all abroad somewhere to dine on hot roast Venison.

Yet even in the midst of jollity, Franklin could not resist a political squib against anti-American policy. Parliament repealed taxes on everything but tea, but still the tea tax ignited mob violence in New York and Boston. In the *Craven Street Gazette,* a correspondent aptly named "Indignation," erupted with a few timely epithets.

Tuesday, 25 September. To the Publisher of the Craven Street Gazette.

Sir,

I make no doubt of the Truth of what the Papers tell us, that a certain great *Person* has been half-starved on the bare Bladebone, *of a Sheep* (I cannot call it *of Mutton* because none was on it) by a Set of the most careless, thoughtless, inconsiderate, corrupt, ignorant, blundering, foolish, crafty, and Knavish Ministers, that ever got into a House and pretended to govern a Family and provide a Dinner. Alas, for the poor Old England of Craven Street! If these nefarious Wretches continue in Power another Week, the Nation will be ruined—Undone!—totally undone, if the Queen does not return; or (which is better) turn them all out and appoint me and my Friends to succeed them.

In an outburst against the London press, "A Hater of Scandal" covers Franklin's backside against criminal libel with a veneer of ironical flattery.

Sir,

Your Correspondent *Indignation* has made a fine Story in your Paper against our excellent Cravenstreet Ministry, as if they meant to starve his Highness, giving him only a bare Blade Bone for his Dinner, while they riot upon roast Venison, &c. The Wickedness of Writers in this Age is truly amazing! I believe we never had since the Foundation of our State, a more faithful, upright, worthy, careful, considerate, incorrupt, discreet, wise, prudent and beneficent Ministry than the present. But if even the Angel Gabriel would condescend to be our Minister and provide our Dinners, he could scarcely escape Newspaper Defamation from a Gang of hungry ever-restless, discontented and malicious Scribblers. It is, Sir, a piece of Justice you owe our righteous Administration to undeceive the Publick on this [Occasion], by assuring them the Fact, which is, that there was provided, and actually smoaking on the Table under his Royal Nose at the same Instant, as fine a Piece of Ribbs of Beef, roasted, as ever Knife was put into; with Potatoes, Horse radish, pickled Walnuts, &c. which Beef his Highness might have eaten of, if so he had pleased to do; and which he forbore to do, merely from a whimsical Opinion (with Respect be it spoken) that Beef doth not with him perspire well, but makes his Back itch, to his no small vexation, now that he hath lost the little Chinese Ivory Hand the End of a Stick, commonly called a *Scratchback*, presented to him by her

Majesty. This is the Truth; and if your boasted Impartiality is real, you will not hesitate a Moment to insert this Letter in your very next Paper. . . .

Marriages. None since our last; but Puss begins to go a Courting.

Deaths. In the back Closet, and elsewhere, many poor Mice.

Stocks. Biscuit very low. Buckwheat and Indian meal, both sour. Tea, lowering daily in the Canister.[21]

Letters overseas to Philadelphia were subject to loss, search, or seizure, so Franklin's familiar letters were more circumspect. He entertained wife Deborah Franklin with occasional apologues, as in teasing her about spoiling daughter Sally's year-old baby, Benjamin Franklin Bache.

It was very prudently done of you not to interfere when his mother thought fit to correct him; which pleases me the more, as I feared, from your Fondness of him, that he would be too much humoured, and perhaps spoiled. There is a Story of two little Boys in the Street; one was crying bitterly; the other came to him to ask what was the Matter? I have been, says he, for a pennyworth of Vinegar, and I have broke the Glass and spilt the Vinegar, and my Mother will whip me. *No, she won't whip you* says the other. Indeed she will, says he. *What,* says the other, have you then got ne'er a Grandmother?[22]

Franklin squeezed this sort of recreational writing in between duties as agent for Georgia, New Jersey, and Massachusetts as well as Pennsylvania. When his closely reasoned arguments had little effect on the policies of Secretary of State for the Colonies Lord Hillsborough, he tried a simpler attack with "New Fables, humbly inscribed to the S—y of St—e for the American Department." Slyly pointing out how previous policies had failed, the fables appeared in the *Public Advertiser* as if a warning that friction between Bostonians and British troops would erupt two months later in the Boston Massacre.

Fable I

A Herd of Cows had long afforded Plenty of Milk, Butter and Cheese to an avaritious Farmer, who grudged them the Grass they subsisted on, and at length mowed it to make Money of the Hay, leaving them to *shift for Food* as they could, and yet still expected to *milk them* as before; but the Cows, offended with his Unreasonableness, resolved for the future *to suckle one another.*

Fable II

An Eagle, King of Birds, sailing on his Wings aloft over a Farmer's Yard, saw a Cat there basking in the Sun, *mistook it for a Rabbit,* stoop'd, seized it, and carried it up into the Air, *intending to prey on it.* The Cat turning, set her Claws into the Eagle's Breast; who, finding his Mistake, opened his Talons, and would have let her drop; but Puss, unwilling to fall so far, held faster; and the Eagle, to get rid of the Inconvenience, found it necessary to *set her down where he took her up.*

Fable III

A Lion's Whelp was put on board a Guinea Ship bound to America as a present to a Friend in that Country: It was tame and harmless as a Kitten, and therefore not confined, but suffered to walk about the Ship at Pleasure. A stately, full-grown English Mastiff, belonging to the Captain, despising the Weakness of the young Lion, frequently took it's *Food* by Force, and often turned it out of its Lodging Box, when he had a Mind to repose therein himself. The young Lion nevertheless grew daily in Size and Strength, and the Voyage being long, he became at last a more equal Match for the Mastiff; who continuing his Insults, received a stunning Blow from the Lion's Paw that fetched his Skin over his Ears, and deterred him from any future Contest with such growing Strength; regretting that he had not rather secured it's Friendship than provoked it's Enmity.[23]

Offsetting anti-American policies were Franklin's friends, who organized in opposition to the Ministry's administration. One, Jonathan Shipley, Bishop of St. Asaph, spoke for America in the House of Lords. It was at the Bishop's estate in August 1771 that Franklin found a fortnight's rest and recreation, with leisure enough to begin writing his autobiography. His reenergized spirits were reflected in a thank-you letter written to the Shipleys recording a delightful conversation en route to London with eleven-year-old Kitty Shipley, who was then returning to school. The letter is another instance showing Franklin enjoying private humor for its own sake, without some ultimate aim in view other than sharing the fun.

The first Stage we were rather pensive. I tried several Topics of Conversation, but none of them would hold. But after Breakfast, we began to recover Spirits, and had a good deal of Chat. . . . We talk'd of her [twenty-six-year-old] Brother, and she wish'd he was married. And don't you wish your Sisters married too? Yes. All but [twenty-one-year-old] Emily; I would not have her married. Why? Because I can't spare her, I can't part with her. The rest may marry as soon as they please, so they do but get good Husbands. We then took upon us to consider for 'em what sort of Husbands would be fittest for every one of them. . . .

[They dispose of fifteen-year-old Georgiana to a squire and seventeen-year-old Betsy to a merchant.—] We proceeded to Emily, her dear Emily, I was afraid we should hardly find any thing good enough for Emily; but at last, after first settling that, if she did marry, Kitty was to live a good deal with her; we agreed that as Emily was very handsome we might expect an Earl for her: So having fix'd her, as I thought, a Countess, we went on to [twenty-three-year-old] Anna-Maria. She, says Kitty, should have a rich Man that has a large Family and a great many things to take care of; for she is very good at managing, helps my Mama very much, can look over Bills, and order all sorts of Family Business. Very well; and as there is a Grace and Dignity in her Manner that would become the Station, what do you think of giving her a Duke? O no! I'll have the Duke for Emily. You may give the Earl to Anna-Maria if you please: But Emily shall have the Duke. I contested this Matter some time; but at length was forc'd to give up the point, leave Emily in Possession of the Duke, and content myself with the Earl for Anna Maria.

And now what shall we do for Kitty? We have forgot her, all this Time. Well, and what will you do for her? I suppose that tho' the rest have resolv'd against the Army, she may not yet have made so rash a Resolution. Yes, but she has: Unless, now, an old one, an old General that has done fighting, and is rich, such a one as General Rufane; I like him a good deal; You must know I like an old Man, indeed I do: And some how or other all the old Men take to me, all that come to our House like me better than my other Sisters: I go to 'em and ask 'em how they do, and they like it mightily; and the Maids take notice of it, and say when they see an old Man come, there's a Friend of yours, Miss Kitty. But then as you like an old General, hadn't you better take him while he's a young Officer, and let him grow old upon your Hands, because then, you'll like him better and better every Year as he grows older and older. No, that won't do. He must be an old Man of 70 or 80, and take me when I am about 30: And then you know I may be a rich young Widow. [She died at age eighty-one, unwed.][24]

Conscious of being caught at the leading edge of an impending tempest, Franklin still found time for another humorous letter for the Shipleys memorializing the death of Mungo, alias Skugg, their pet squirrel. Unlike the earlier, better-known but apolitical epitaph of his own, the formal lament for Mungo may be read as a stealth fable for those Americans who were demanding full freedom too soon.

I lament with you most sincerely the unfortunate End of poor *Mungo:* Few Squirrels were better accomplish'd; for he had had a good Education, had travell'd far, and seen much of the World. As he had the Honour of being for his Virtues your Favourite, he should not go like common Skuggs [pet squirrels] without an Elegy or an Epitaph. Let us give him one in the monumental Stile and Measure, which being neither Prose nor Verse, is perhaps the properest for Grief; since to use common Language would look as if we were not affected, and to make Rhimes would seem Trifling in Sorrow.

Alas! poor *Mungo!*
Happy wert thou, hadst thou known
Thy own Felicity!
Remote from the fierce Bald-Eagle
Tyrant of thy native Woods,
Thou hadst nought to fear from his piercing Talons;
Nor from the murdering Gun
Of the thoughtless Sportsman.
Safe in thy wired Castle,
Grimalkin never could annoy thee.
Daily wert thou fed with the choicest Viands
By the fair Hand
Of an indulgent Mistress.
But, discontented, thou wouldst have more Freedom.
Too soon, alas! didst thou obtain it,
And, wandering
Fell by the merciless Fangs,
Of wanton, cruel Ranger [a pet dog].
Learn hence, ye who blindly wish more Liberty,
Whether Subjects, Sons, Squirrels or Daughters,
That apparent *Restraint* may be real *Protection,*
Yielding Peace, Plenty, and Security.

You see how much more decent and proper this broken Stile, interrupted as it were with Sighs, is for the Occasion, than if one were to say, by way of Epitaph,

Here Skugg
Lies snug
As a Bug
In a Rug.

And yet perhaps there are People in the World of so little Feeling as to think, *that* would be a good-enough Epitaph for our poor Mungo![25]

With a change in administration that saw antagonist Lord Hillsborough replaced as colonial secretary, Franklin looked forward to a more friendly climate. He was poised to play a leading role in reconciling the new Ministry and the American colonies. But he had been too far and too long away from Boston to sense the turmoil and temper of the American people. Franklin made an egregious error. Thinking that he would pour a little oil on troubled waters, he sent to Bostonians by way of reassuring them of their rectitude a packet of intercepted private letters from their governor, Thomas Hutchinson, who was urging harsher restrictions. The firestorm that erupted would leave him publicly disgraced, discharged from public service, and designated in the House of Lords as "One of the bitterest and most mischievous Enemies this Country had ever known."[26] But he stood his ground. He would use a pen forged in forty years of newspaper wars as a lever to move the world.

6

Losing London

1773–1776

In the crucial years leading to America's break with Britain, Franklin carried the burden of reconciliation. In June 1773 the Hutchinson letters he had sent to Boston provoked Massachusetts to petition the king for the governor's removal. It was up to agent Franklin to submit the inflammatory petition to the Privy Council. They delayed for months before setting a hearing date. Franklin chafed at their disrespect and his defamation in their partisan press. "Tir'd of Meekness," he used his satire to hold up "a Looking-Glass in which some Ministers may see their ugly Faces, and the Nation its Injustice."[1]

In the *Public Advertiser* (11 September 1773), Franklin impersonated archconservative "Q.E.D." who proposed a set of twenty "Rules by Which a Great Empire May be Reduced to a Small One"—an ironic litany of America's grievances that anticipated in its particularized complaints the Declaration of Independence. Franklin, who had used the popular recipe formula in Silence Dogood's "Receipt to make a New-England Funeral Elegy," applied it now to the high crimes and misdemeanors of unindicted coconspirators in the Ministry. The tone of the whole is more invective than ironic. Taking the premises of colonial policy to their logical extreme in the manner of Jonathan Swift, Franklin narrowed his focus by subtitling the article, "Presented privately to a *late Minister,* when he entered upon his Administration," as if these had been the rules Lord Hillsborough had followed. Franklin included such other political targets as former Massachusetts governor Francis Bernard, whose bad advice on American affairs had been rewarded with a baronetcy. Such personal animosity made it difficult for Franklin to dissemble frustration and disgust. Too bitter, he confined humor to the opening passages excerpted below. The opening is a subtle allusion to Francis Bacon, one of Franklin's heroes. Bacon attributes the saying about fiddling and nation building to Themistocles in the popular essay, "Of the True Greatness of Kingdoms and Estates,"[2] especially pertinent here since it too offers a recipe for the "amplitude and greatness" of a kingdom.

An ancient Sage valued himself upon this, that tho' he could not fiddle, he knew how to make a *great City* of a *little one.* The Science that I, a modern Simpleton, am about to communicate is the very reverse.

I address myself to all Ministers who have the Management of extensive Dominions, which from their very Greatness are become troublesome to govern, because the Multiplicity of their Affairs leaves no Time for *fiddling.*

I. In the first Place, Gentlemen, you are to consider, that a great Empire, like a great Cake, is most easily diminished at the Edges. Turn your Attention therefore first to your remotest Provinces; that as you get rid of them, the next may follow in Order.

II. That the Possibility of this Separation may always exist, take special Care the Provinces are never incorporated with the Mother Country, that they do not enjoy the same common Rights, the same Privileges in Commerce, and that they are governed by *severer* Laws, all of *your enacting,* without allowing them any Share in the Choice of the Legislators. By carefully making and preserving such Distinctions, you will (to keep to my Simile of the Cake) act like a wise Gingerbread Baker, who, to facilitate a Division, cuts his Dough half through in those Places, where, when bak'd, he would have it *broken to Pieces.* . . .

IV. However peaceably your Colonies have submitted to your Government, shewn their Affection to your Interest, and patiently borne their Grievances, you are to *suppose* them always inclined to revolt, and treat them accordingly. Quarter Troops among them, who by their Insolence may *provoke* the rising of Mobs, and by their Bullets and Bayonets suppress them. By this Means, like the Husband who uses his Wife ill *from Suspicion*, you may in Time convert your *Suspicions* into *Realities*. . . .

VII. When . . . Governors have crammed their Coffers, and made themselves so odious to the People that they can no longer remain among them with Safety to their Persons, recall and *reward* them with Pensions. You may make them *Baronets* too, if that respectable Order should not think fit to resent it. . . .

IX. Remember to make your arbitrary Tax more grievous to your Provinces, by public Declarations importing that your Power of taxing them has *no limits*, so that when you take from them without their Consent a Shilling in the Pound, you have a clear Right to the other nineteen. This will probably weaken every idea of *Security in their Property*, and convince them that under such a Government *they have nothing they can call their own*; which can scarce fail of producing *the happiest Consequences!*. . . .

XVI. Believe nothing you hear from the Friends of the People. Suppose all *their* Complaints to be invented and promoted by a few factious Demagogues, whom if you could catch and hang, all would be quiet. Catch and hang a few of them accordingly; and the *Blood of the Martyrs* shall *work Miracles* in favour of your Purpose. . . .

XIX. Send Armies into their Country under Pretence of protecting the Inhabitants; but instead of garrisoning the Forts on their Frontiers with those Troops, to prevent Incursions, demolish those Forts, and order the Troops into the Heart of the Country, that the Savages may be encouraged to attack the Frontiers, and that the Troops may be protected by the Inhabitants: This will seem to proceed from your Ill will or your Ignorance, and contribute farther to produce and strengthen an Opinion among them, *that you are no longer fit to govern them*.

XX. Lastly, Invest the General of your Army in the Provinces with great and unconstitutional Powers, and free him from the Controul of even your own Civil Governors. Let him have Troops enow under his Command, with all the Fortresses in his Possession; and who knows but (like some provincial Generals in the Roman Empire, and encouraged by the universal Discontent you have produced) he may take it into his Head to set up for himself. If he should, and you have carefully practised these few *excellent Rules* of mine, take my Word for it, all the Provinces will immediately join him, and you will that Day (If you have not done it sooner) get rid of the Trouble of governing them, and all the *Plagues* attending their *Commerce* and Connection from thenceforth and for ever.[3]

A fortnight later, the *Public Advertiser* printed Franklin's satiric masterpiece, the "Edict by the King of Prussia" (22 September 1773). In submitting it to the editor, his friend Henry Sampson Woodfall, Franklin asked him "to take Care that the Compositor observes strictly the Italicking, Capitalling and Pointing."[4] The reason was that the "Edict" exactly followed the legal form of a Parliamentary measure. Its five sections adapted, mostly word for word, the pertinent British laws that restricted American manufacturing and shipping of iron and steel, exporting wool, making hats, and mandating transportation of felons to America.[5] Woodfall printed the "Edict" on page one as "Foreign Intelligence," giving it awesome authenticity. Frederick the Great, with the finest army in Europe, had been an immanent threat since May 1762 when Britain, then an ally, secretly tried to split Prussia's friendship with Russia. Ten years later, the hapless British could only watch as Prussia, Russia, and Austria dismembered Poland and Frederick occupied the vital port of Danzig. In September 1773, fearful rumors spread that Frederick was about to embargo British shipping at that port. At the same time, the press debated his claim to that city as direct descendant of a sixteenth-century Teutonic knight.[6] The unspoken fear was that he would make a similar claim to Great Britain through his mother's brother, George I.

Dantzick, September 5

We have long wondered here at the Supineness of the English Nation, under the Prussian Impositions upon its Trade entering our Port. We did not till lately know the *Claims,* antient and modern, that hang over that Nation, and therefore could not suspect that it might submit to those Impositions from a Sense of *Duty,* or from Principles of *Equity* The following *Edict,* just made public, may, if serious, throw some Light upon this Matter.

"Frederick, by the Grace of God, King of Prussia, &c. &c. &c. to all present and to come, **Health**. The Peace now enjoyed throughout our Dominions, having afforded us Leisure to apply ourselves to the Regulation of Commerce, the Improvement of our Finances, and at the same Time the easing our *Domestic Subjects* in their Taxes: For these Causes, and other good Considerations us thereunto moving, We hereby make known, that after having deliberated these Affairs in our Council, present our dear Brothers, and other great Officers of the State, Members of the same, **We** of our certain Knowledge, full Power and Authority Royal, have made and issued this present Edict, viz.

"**Whereas** it is well known to all the World, that the first German Settlements made in the Island of Britain, were by Colonies of People, Subjects to our renowned Ducal Ancestors, and drawn from *their* Dominions, under the Conduct of Hengist, Horsa, Hella, Uffa, Cerdicus, Ida, and others; and that the said Colonies have flourished under the Protection of our august House, for Ages past, have never been *emancipated* therefrom, and yet have hitherto yielded little Profit to the same. And whereas We Ourself have in the last War fought for and defended the said Colonies against the Power of France, and thereby enabled them to make Conquests from the said Power in America, for which we have not yet received adequate Compensation. And whereas it is just and expedient that a Revenue should be raised from the said Colonies in Britain towards our Indemnification; and that those who are Descendants of our antient Subjects, and thence still owe us due Obedience, should contribute to the replenishing of our Royal

Coffers, as they must have done had their Ancestors remained in the Territories now to us appertaining: **We** do therefore hereby ordain and command, That from and after the Date of these Presents, there shall be levied and paid to our Officers of the Customs, on all Goods, Wares and Merchandizes, and on all Grain and other Produce of the Earth exported from the said Island of Britain, and on all Goods of whatever Kind imported into the same, a *Duty* of *Four and an Half* per Cent. *ad Valorem,* for the Use of us and our Successors. And that the said Duty may more effectually be collected, *We* do hereby ordain, that all Ships or Vessels bound from Great Britain to any other Part of the World, or from any other Part of the World to Great Britain, shall in their respective Voyages touch at our Port of **Koningsberg**, there to be unladen, searched, and charged with the said Duties."

> Franklin ironically abstracts resurrected laws against iron mining and manufacturing. His effect is to focus on Americans presuming that "they had a natural Right to make the best Use they could of the natural productions of their Country for their own benefit." He next reproduces a Rabelaisian catalogue of actual wool trade regulations, adding such touches as the prohibition of carrying wool "even across the smallest River or Creek."

"We do hereby absolutely forbid the Transportation of Wool from thence even to the Mother Country Prussia; and that those Islanders may be farther and more effectually restrained in making any Advantage of their own Wool in the Way of Manufacture, We command that none shall be carried *out of one County into another,* nor shall any Worsted-Bay, or Woolen-Yarn, Cloth, Says, Bays, Kerseys, Serges, Frizes, Druggets, Cloth-Serges, Shalloons, or any other Drapery Stuffs, or Woolen Manufactures whatsoever, made up or mixt with Wool in any of the said Counties, be carried into any other County, or be Waterborne even across the smallest River or Creek, on Penalty of Forfeiture of the same, together with the Boats, Carriages, Horses, &c. that shall be employed in removing them. *Nevertheless* Our loving Subjects there are hereby permitted,(if they think proper) to use all their Wool as *Manure for the Improvement of their Lands."*

Except for reemphasizing Americans' presumption of a natural right to their own production, Franklin takes the premises of regulating the hat industry to their absurd conclusion.

"**And whereas** the Art and Mystery of making *Hats* hath arrived at great Perfection in Prussia, and the making of Hats by our remote Subjects ought to be as much as possible restrained. And forasmuch as the Islanders before-mentioned, being in Possession of Wool, Beaver, and other Furs, have *presumptuously* conceived they had a Right to make some Advantage thereof, by manufacturing the same into Hats, to the Prejudice of our domestic Manufacture, **We** do therefore hereby strictly command and ordain, that no Hats or Felts whatsoever, dyed or undyed, finished or unfinished, shall be loaden or put into or upon any Vessel, Cart, Carriage or Horse, to be transported or conveyed *out of one County* in the said Island *into another County,* or to *any other Place whatsoever,* by any Person or Persons whatsoever, on Pain of forfeiting the same, with a Penalty of *Five Hundred Pounds* Sterling for every Offence. Nor shall any Hat-maker in any of the said Counties employ more than two Apprentices, on penalty of *Five Pounds* Sterling per Month: We intending hereby that such Hatmakers, being so restrained both in the Production and Sale of their Commodity, may find no Advantage in continuing their Business. But lest the said Islanders should suffer Inconveniency by the Want of Hats, We are farther graciously pleased to permit them to send their Beaver Fur to Prussia; and We also permit Hats made thereof to be exported from Prussia to Britain, the People thus favoured to pay all Costs and Charges of Manufacturing, Interest, Commission to our Merchants, Insurance and Freight going and returning, as in the Case of Iron.

"And lastly, Being willing farther to favour Our said Colonies in *Britain,* We do hereby also ordain and command, that all the Thieves, Highway and Street-Robbers, House-breakers, Forgerers,

Murderers, So[dom]ites, and Villains of every Denomination, who have forfeited their Lives to the Law in Prussia, but whom We, in Our great Clemency, do not think fit here to hang, shall be emptied out of our Gaols into the said Island of Great Britain *for the* ***better Peopling*** *of that Country.*

"We flatter Ourselves that these Our Royal Regulations and Commands will be thought *just* and *reasonable* by Our much-favoured Colonists in England, the said Regulations being copied from their own Statutes of 10 and 11 Will. III. C. 10 [tenth and eleventh years of the reign of William III, chapter 10], 5 Geo. II. C. 22, 23 Geo. II. C. 29, 4 Geo. I. C.11, and from other equitable Laws made by their Parliaments, or from Instructions given by their Princes, or from Resolutions of both Houses entered into for the **Good *Government*** of their own Colonies in Ireland and America."

Having satirized old laws recently revived, Franklin brings his catalog of unconstitutional laws up to date with the most timely outrage, voiced also in "Rules by Which a Great Empire May be Reduced." After Rhode Island patriots burned the revenue schooner *Gaspé,* Parliament resolved that the culprits be brought to England for trial.

"And all Persons in the said island are hereby cautioned not to oppose in any wise the Execution of this Our Edict, or any Part thereof, such Opposition being ***High Treason,*** of which all who are *suspected* shall be transported in Fetters from Britain to Prussia, there to be tried and executed according to the *Prussian Law.*

Such is our Pleasure, Given at Potsdam this twenty-fifth Day of the Month of August, One Thousand Seven Hundred and Seventy-three, and in the Thirty-third Year of our Reign.

By the King in his Council

RECHTMAESSIG, Secr."

Some take this Edict to be merely one of the King's *Jeux d'Esprit:* Others suppose it serious, and that he means a Quarrel with England: But all here think the Assertion it concludes with, "that these Regulations are copied from Acts of the English Parliament respecting their Colonies," a very *injurious* one: it being impossible to believe, that a People distinguish'd for their *Love of Liberty,* a Nation so *wise,* so *liberal in its Sentiments,* so *just and equitable* towards its *Neighbours,* should, from mean and *injudicious* Views of *petty immediate Profit,* treat *its own Children* in a Manner so *arbitrary* and **Tyrannical**![7]

Franklin enjoyed the popular reception of both the "Edict" and the "Rules." Despite a foreboding of the consequences, hubris prevailed. "Those Papers," Franklin told his sister, "have been much taken Notice of, many are pleased with them, and a few very angry, who I am told will make me feel their Resentment, which I must bear as well as I can, and shall bear the better if any publick Good is done, whatever the Consequence to myself."[8] In the meantime, he enjoyed fooling even friends, including the entourage attached to Francis Dashwood, Baron LeDespencer, whose defunct Hell-Fire Club had once enrolled such powerful persons as Prime Minister Lord Bute. Now retired, reformed, and Franklin's patron in the Post Office, Lord LeDespencer had asked his help in abridging the Book of Common Prayer, which they were completing in September 1773 at LeDespencer's estate. Franklin was particularly pleased at the "Edict's" effect on Lord LeDespencer's veteran right-hand man, Paul Whitehead.

What made it the more noticed here was, that the people in reading it, were, as the phrase is, *taken in,* till they had got half through it, and imagined it a real edict, to which mistake I suppose the king of Prussia's *character* must have contributed. I was down at Lord LeDespencer's when the post brought that day's papers. Mr. [Paul] Whitehead was there too . . . who runs early through all the papers, and tells the company what he finds remarkable. He had them in another room, and we were chatting in the breakfast parlour, when he came running in to us, out of breath, with the paper in his hand. "Here!" says he, "here's *news* for ye!

Here's the king of Prussia, claiming a right to this kingdom!" All stared, and I as much as any body; and he went on to read it.

When he had read two or three paragraphs, a gentleman present said, *"Damn his impudence, I dare say, we shall hear by next post that he is upon his march with one hundred thousand men to back this."*

Whitehead, who is very shrewd, soon after began to smoke it, and looking in my face said, *"I'll be hanged if this is not some of your American jokes upon us!"* The reading went on, and ended with abundance of laughing, and a general verdict that it was a fair hit: and the piece was cut out of the paper and preserved in my lord's collection.[9]

Franklin himself preferred the simpler, more conventional style of the "Rules." Yet he saw the "Edict" prove the more effective—"the keenest and severest piece" in a long time, and as dangerous in "giving here a bad impression of the measures of government; and in the colonies, by encouraging them in their contumacy."[10] He gave these opinions with an air of good humor that masked irritation. When former Massachusetts governor, now Sir Francis Bernard, claimed to represent George III and attacked Franklin as an enemy of "all Government," Franklin reacted with an apologue about a young chimney sweep that he did not publish. It could have applied also to Jonas Hanway's exposé of cruelty to child chimney sweepers being made public in the *Advertiser,* before Parliamentary commissions, and in Hanway's shocking study, *The State of Chimney Sweepers' Young Apprentices* (1773).

This puts one in mind of the Chimney-sweeper condemn'd to be hang'd for Theft, who being charitably visited by a good Clergyman for whom he had work'd, said, *I hope your Honour will take my part, and get a Reprieve for me, and not let my Enemies have their Will; because it is upon your Account that they have prosecuted and sworn against me.* On my Account! How can that be?

Why, Sir, because as how, ever since they knew I was employ'd by your Honour, they resolv'd upon my Ruin: for they are Enemies to all Religion; and they hate you and me and every body in black.[11]

Franklin still displayed congenial good humor for occasional correspondents like fellow scientist William Brownrigg, to whom he had given a favorite recipe for Parmesan cheese. Franklin's culinary joke is that for proper plum pudding, a floured cloth bag is used to boil the mash of fruit, eggs, bread, brandy, etc., just as in making Parmesan cheese a cloth bag is used to squeeze the whey from the curds.

I suppose Mrs. Brownrigg did not succeed in making the Parmesan Cheese, since we have heard nothing of it. But as a Philosophess, she will not be discouraged by one or two Failures. Perhaps some Circumstance is omitted in the Receipt, which by a little more Experience she may discover. The foreign Gentleman, who had learnt in England to like boiled Plumbpudding, and carried home a Receipt for making it, wondered to see it brought to his Table in the Form of a Soup. The Cook declar'd he had exactly followed the Receipt. And when that came to be examined, a small, but important Circumstance appeared to have been omitted. There was no Mention of the Bag.[12]

Events moved too swiftly for lasting good humor. Christmas 1773, the *Advertiser* published Franklin's confession that he alone was responsible for obtaining and sending Governor Hutchinson's letters to Boston. The confession gave his antagonists their opening. On 10 January 1774, on the pretext of hearing Massachusetts's petition to replace Hutchinson, the Privy Council summoned Franklin to public display at the Cockpit where there was ample room for spectators. Realizing that he would need an attorney, Franklin obtained a postponement until the 29th. But on the 24th, the *Advertiser* reported news of the Boston Tea Party. After five days of public outrage, the hearing on the Massachusetts petition opened to a full house crammed with spectators eager to see Franklin flayed in order to preserve "the Dependence of the Colonies on the Mother Country."[13]

Hearing the petition was mere pretext, the Privy Council's immediate aim was to destroy Franklin as source and symbol of

American insurrection. To raucous laughter and applause, prosecutor Alexander Wedderburn spewed a stream of insults. The climax came as Wedderburn, focusing on the stolen Hutchinson letters, branded Franklin a real "Homo trium literarum" [a man of letters]—the letters "t h i e f." Two weeks later in the *Advertiser,* Franklin countered with white-hot irony in a letter as from "Homo Trium Literarum."

The Admirers of Dr. Franklin in England are much shocked at Mr. Wedderburne's calling him a Thief; but perhaps they will be less surprised at this Circumstance when they are informed, that his greatest Admirers on the Continent agree in entertaining the same Idea of him. As an Evidence of this, I send you a Copy of a poetical Stanza, which is engraved under his Portrait prefixed to the late French Translation of his Work, in two Volumes, Quarto.

I shall also send you an Attempt of a Translation of them, that the English Reader may be able to judge of the Similarity between the Idea of Mr. Wedderburne and that of the French Philosopher [A-R-J Turgot], with whom all the Philosophers in Europe intirely concur. It will even be seen that Foreigners represent him as much more impudent and audacious in his Thefts than the English Orator (though he was under no Restraint from a Regard to Truth) has ventured to insinuate.

Il a ravi le feu des cieux,
Il fait fleurir les arts en des climats sauvages.
L'Amerique le place a la tête des sages,
La Grece l'auroit mis au nombre de ses Dieux.

In English:

To steal from Heaven its sacred Fire he taught,
The Arts to thrive in savage Climes he brought:
In the New World the first of Men esteem'd;
Among the Greeks a God he had been deem'd.[14]

Again in the *Advertiser* (17 May 1774), Franklin attacked the Ministry with only thinly veiled contempt. In proposing "A Method of Humbling Rebellious American Vassals," he posed as "A Freeholder of Old Sarum," a "pocket borough" notorious as a seat in Parliament representing nobody but its proprietor. The Freeholder proposes a remedy that Franklin had earlier overheard from a British officer.[15] Now apparently propelled by the mechanical operation of the spirit in which soul and common sense are put on hold, Freeholder delved to the root of rebellion.

As we have declared by our Representatives that we are the supreme Lords of their Persons and Property, and their occupying our Territory at such a remote Distance without a proper Controul from us, except at a very great Expence, encourages a mutinous Disposition, and may, if not timely prevented, dispose them in perhaps less than a Century to deny our Authority, slip their Necks out of the Collar, and from being Slaves set up for Masters, more especially when it is considered that they are a robust, hardy People, encourage early Marriages, and their Women being amazingly prolific, they must of consequence in 100 Years be very numerous, and of course be able to set us at defiance. Effectually to prevent which, as have an undoubted Right to do, it is humbly proposed, and we do hereby give it as Part of our Instructions to our Representatives, that a Bill be brought in and passed, and Orders immediately transmitted to G[ener]al G[ag]e, our Commander in Chief in North America, in consequence of it, that all the Males there be c[a]st[rat]ed.

He may make a Progress thro' the several Towns of North America at the Head of five Batallions, which we hear our experienced Generals, who have been consulted, think sufficient to subdue America if they were in open Rebellion; for who can resist the intrepid Sons of Britain, the Terror of France and Spain, and the Conquerors of America in Germany [in the Seven Years' War]. Let a Company of Sow-gelders, consisting of 100 Men, accompany the Army. On their Arrival at any Town or Village, let Orders be given that on the blowing of the Horn all the Males be assembled in the Market Place. If the Corps are Men of Skill and Ability in their Profession, they will make great Dispatch, and retard but very little the Progress of the Army.

There may be a Clause in the Bill to be left at the Discretion of the General, whose Powers ought to be very extensive, that the most notorious Offenders, such as Hancock, Adams, &c. who have been the Ringleaders in the Rebellion of our Servants, should be shaved quite close. But that none of the Offenders may escape in the Town of Boston, let all the Males there suffer the latter Operation, as it will be conformable to the modern Maxim that is now generally adopted by our worthy Constituents, that it is better that ten innocent Persons should suffer than that one guilty should escape. It is true, Blood will be shed, but probably not many Lives lost. Bleeding to a certain Degree is salutary. The English, whose Humanity is celebrated by all the World, but particularly by themselves, do not desire the Death of the Delinquent, but his Reformation.

The Advantages arising from this Scheme being carried into Execution are obvious. In the Course of fifty Years it is probable we shall not have one rebellious Subject in North America. This will be laying the Axe to the Root of the Tree. In the mean time a considerable Expence may be saved to the Managers of the Opera, and our Nobility and Gentry may be entertained at a cheaper Rate by the fine Voices of our own C[a]st[rat]i, and the Specie remain in the Kingdom, which now, to an enormous Amount, is carried every Year to Italy. It might likewise be of Service to our Levant Trade, as we could supply the Grand Signor's Seraglio, and the Harams of the Grandees of the Turkish Dominions with Cargos of Eunuchs, as also with handsome Women, for which America is as famous as Circassia. I could enumerate many other Advantages. I shall mention but one: It would effectually put a Stop to the Emigrations from this Country now grown so very fashionable.[16]

Franklin tried unsuccessfully to disguise his cold fury behind a parody of overheated revenge tragedies popular on the London stage. In an unsigned paper meant for the *Advertiser,* he paraded public accusations of his "Ingratitude to the Ministry of this

Nation, who have conferred upon him so many Favours." Perhaps Franklin did not finish the paper because its self-revealing invective erased the ironic distance that had made the "Edict" or the "Rules" so effective.

They gave him the Post Office in America; they made his Son a Governor; and they offer'd him a Post of five hundred a Year in the [revenue] Salt Office, if he would relinquish the Interests of his Countrey; but he has had the Wickedness to continue true to it, and is as much an American as ever. As it is a settled Point in Government here, that every Man has his Price, 'tis plain they are Bunglers in their Business, and have not given him enough. Their Master has as much reason to be angry with them as Rodrigue in the Play, with his Apothecary for not effectually poisoning Pandolpho, and they must probably make use of the Apothecary's Justification; Viz.

Scene 4th
Rodrigue and *Fell* the Apothecary.

Rodrigue. You promised to have this Pandolpho upon his Bier in less than a Week; 'Tis more than a Month since, and he still walks and stares me in the Face.

Fell. True: and yet I have done my best Endeavours. In various Ways I have given the Miscreant as much Poison as would have kill'd an Elephant. He has swallow'd Dose after Dose; far from hurting him, he seems the better for it. He hath a wonderfully strong Constitution. I find I cannot kill him but by cutting his Throat, and that, as I take it, is not my Business.

Rodrigue. Then it must be mine.[17]

His intimate friend Joseph Priestley revealed Franklin's low-grade depression at this time. On their last day together in London, as Franklin read about the effects of Parliament's revenge on Boston, tears literally ran down his cheeks.[18] Was it for this that he had suffered accusation of treason, public disgrace, loss of the post office, and failure as negotiator? Ultimately, he maintained that the death of his wife Deborah at sixty-six determined him to leave England. She had managed their business in his absence. In forty-four years of marriage, he had been absent half the time. Sailing home (20 March–5 May 1775) gave him the chance to relive their courtship in his memoirs and find relief in recollecting such pranks as he had played on his early employer Samuel Keimer. One of the memoir's comical highlights recalls how Franklin persuaded "great Gourmandizer" Keimer to join him in a vegetarian diet.[19]

The memoirs also gave him the chance to laugh at himself practicing self-delusion, the controlling idea behind Franklin's satirizing the mechanical operation of the spirit and more seriously the abuse of reason.

I believe I have omitted mentioning that in my first Voyage from Boston, being becalm'd off Block Island, our People set about catching Cod & hawl'd up a great many. Hitherto I had stuck to my Resolution of not eating animal Food; and on this Occasion, I consider'd with my Master Tryon, the taking every Fish as a kind of Murder, since none of them had or ever could do us any Injury that might justify the Slaughter. All this was very reasonable. But I had formerly been a great Lover of Fish, & when this came out of the Frying Pan, it smelt admirably well. I balanc'd some time between Principle & Inclination: At length I recollected, that when the Fish were opened, I saw smaller Fish taken out of their Stomachs: Then, thought I, if you eat one another, I don't see why we may n't eat you. So I din'd upon Cod very heartily and continu'd to eat with other People, returning only now & then to a vegetable Diet. So convenient a thing it is to be a *reasonable Creature,* since it enables one to find or make a Reason for every thing one has a mind to do.[20]

Franklin arrived home on 20 March to find Philadelphia in a frenzy—arming, drilling, still arguing reconciliation. The next day, neighbors elected him to Congress as a septuagenarian security blanket against an uncertain future.

7

Seducing Paris

1776–1782

Coming home to Philadelphia on 5 May 1775 allowed Franklin no time for comedy. On the following day, his neighbors elected him to the Continental Congress. In November, Congress dispatched him to confer with General Washington at Cambridge. The next spring, they sent him to Canada to recruit allies. In autumn, he went to Staten Island to negotiate a last time with Lord Richard Howe. In October, he was posted to Paris seeking funds and allies. He arrived on 23 December with two young grandsons, Benjamin Bache and William Temple Franklin, and settled down at suburban Passy where, he said, for the next eight years, he went through more business than ever before in his life.[1]

In America, duty had left no time for writing humorous familiar letters. In France, that sort of personal writing offered a means to learn French, ingratiate himself with the French court, and shape public opinion. His fame as comical Poor Richard, or Bonhomme Richard, preceded him, and so, as in the *Craven Street Gazette,* he put on the Socratic mask as his own comic hero. When illness imposed idleness, or in periods of enforced inaction, he wrote comical letters or short essays, "bagatelles"—little sketches—knowing that they would be read in fashionable salons. In his official capacity, of course, he composed informational brochures on America, but as the principal American bureaucrat, harried by requests, he would find comic relief in such exercises as a letter of recommendation suitable for all occasions.

Paris April 2, 1777

Sir,

The Bearer of this who is going to America, presses me to give him a Letter of Recommendation, tho' I know nothing of him, not even his Name. This may seem extraordinary, but I assure you it is not uncommon here. Sometimes indeed one unknown Person brings me another equally unknown, to recommend him, and sometimes they recommend one another! As to this gentleman, I must refer you to himself for his Character and Merits, with which he is certainly better acquainted than I can possibly be; I recommend him however to those Civilities which every Stranger, of whom one knows no Harm, has a Right to, and I request you will do him all the good Offices and show him all the Favour that on further Acquaintance you shall find him to deserve. I have the honour to be, &c.[2]

Franklin continued to give his comic fancy freest range in familiar letters. To Emma Thompson, an Anglo-Irish friend from London before the war, he described himself pretty much as the Abbé Flamarens described him in the Paris tabloid, *Memoires Secrets* (15 January 1777): carrying a cane, wearing glasses, dressed simply as a Quaker, thin hair unpowdered in a fur cap—a cartoon of Parisian preconceptions of an amiable American Quaker grandpa.

I know you wish you could see me, but as you can't, I will describe my self to you. Figure me in your mind as jolly as formerly, and as strong and hearty, only a few Years older, very plainly dress'd, wearing my thin grey strait Hair, that peeps out under my only Coiffure, a fine Fur Cap, which comes down my Forehead almost to my Spectacles. Think how this must appear among the Powder'd Heads of Paris. I wish every Gentleman and Lady in France would only be so obliging as to follow my Fashion, comb their own Heads as I do mine, dismiss their Friseurs, and pay me half the Money they paid to them. You see the Gentry might well afford this; and I could then inlist those Friseurs, who are at least 100,000; and with the Money I would maintain them, make a Visit with them to England, and dress the Heads of your Ministers and Privy Counsellors, which I conceive to be at present *un peu dérangeés* [a little disordered].[3]

Franklin joked about his iconography in France. Despite rumors that Louis XVI had chamber pots with Franklin's image at the bottom, none survive.[4] In *Memoires Secrets* the Abbé Flamarens reported Franklin's portrait was the favorite New Year's gift and that people kept it on their mantles like an icon. With a little more modesty, Franklin reported the same phenomenon in writing to daughter Sally Bache about his miniature portrait on clay by Jean-Baptiste Nini.

[The medallion] was the first of the kind made in France. A variety of others have been made since of different sizes; some to be set in lids of snuff boxes, and some so small as to be worn in rings; and the numbers sold are incredible. These, with the pictures, busts, and prints, (of which copies upon copies are spread every where) have made your father's face as well known as that of the moon, so that he durst not do any thing that would oblige him to run away, as his phiz would discover him wherever he should venture to show it. It is said by learned etymologists that the name *Doll,* for the images children play with, is derived from the word **Idol**; from the number of *dolls* now made of him, he may truly be said, *in that sense,* to be *i-doll-ized* in this country.[5]

By the close of 1777, idolatry of Franklin had become a French national pastime. The *Pennsylvania Gazette* (31 December 1777) reported Parisians buying places at windows to see him pass by in his coach, trailing crowds of gentility. Salon society lionized him, and women flocked to embrace him. Understanding not a word they said, he would nevertheless greet each as though she were the only woman in the room. They adored him.[6] Wryly, Franklin told his stepniece Elizabeth Partridge how he in his seventies had acquired the reputation of a rake.

> You mention the Kindness of the French Ladies to me. I must explain that matter. This is the civilest Nation upon Earth. Your first Acquaintances endeavour to find out what you like, and they tell others. If 'tis understood that you like Mutton, dine where you will you find Mutton. Somebody, it seems, gave it out that I lov'd Ladies; and then every body presented me their Ladies (or the Ladies presented themselves) to be *embrac'd,* that is to have their Necks kiss'd. For as to kissing of Lips or Cheeks it is not the Mode here; the first is reckon'd rude, & the other may rub off the Paint. The French Ladies have however 1000 other ways of rendering themselves agreable; by their various Attentions and Civilities, & their sensible Conversation. 'Tis a delightful People to live with.[7]

Franklin himself maneuvered that reputation in a public relations campaign that included composing more than a dozen of the little bagatelles. In the style of familiar letters, these could be considered apologues focused on a simple plot meant to make a moral point. As in *les récits* of modern French literature, Franklin impersonated himself recollecting some (usually) humorous experience. His drafts were translated into French by such Parisian friends as Jaques Barbeu-Dubourg, translator of his technical works, or Madame Helvétius. Next, he printed the bagatelles on the private press he used for official forms. He knew that both the bagatelles and the familiar letters would circulate in fashionable salons. Because France's favorite indoor sport was lovemaking, the letters sometimes teetered on the edge of soft-core pornography—as in protesting the reluctance of his lovely neighbor Anne-Louise Brillon de Jouy to satisfy his sexual appetite, where he draws an analogy between Cupid's anatomy and his own organ of venery.

My poor little Boy, whom you ought methinks to have cherish'd, instead of being fat and Jolly like those in your elegant Drawings, is meagre and starv'd almost to death for want of the substantial Nourishment which you his Mother inhumanly deny him, and yet would now clip his little Wings to prevent his seeking it elsewhere![8]

This sort of gallantry earned septuagenarian Franklin everlasting notoriety as a great lover. Gossip claimed he bantered with a beauty who sat upon his lap: "Why," he teased, "have you never invited me to spend the night?" She assured him he could stay that very night. The old man, caught off guard, cleared his throat: "'Tis midsummer's eve. Let us wait until the nights are longer."[9] Rather than repartee, Franklin more often amused the company with homely apologues. When Madame Brillon told him people gossiped about "the sweet habit" she had of sitting on his lap "and your habit of soliciting from me what I always refuse," Franklin countered with a timely apologue.

A beggar asked an Archbishop for an alm of a Louis.—A Louis for a beggar, that would be extravagant!—Just an ecu then.—Still too much.—Let us say a farthing, or your blessing.—My blessing, now, there is a sensible idea.—I don't want it any more, for if it was worth a farthing, you would not give it to me.[10]

Other popular bagatelles dwelt on the irony of love. Franklin returned to the device of a dream vision he had used for Silence Dogood. This time he uses the dream to seduce Madame Helvétius, who objects because of undying love for her late husband. In the Elysian Fields, Franklin tells the late husband's spirit about her undying love, but the spirit replies that he has a new wife, who turns out to be the spirit of Deborah Franklin, Franklin's late wife. Their spirited conversation takes on a neat touch of irony. Did she merely misremember having been a "good wife forty-nine years and four months"? Or had Franklin forgotten their anniversary?

I reclaimed to her. But she told me coldly, "I have been your good wife forty-nine years and four months, nearly a half century; be content with that. Here I have formed a new connection, which will endure to eternity."

Resigned to flesh over spirit, Franklin returns to Madame Helvétius and ends with a proposition.

Offended by this refusal of my Eurydice, I suddenly decided to leave these ungrateful spirits, to return to the good earth, to see again the sunshine and you. Here I am! Let us revenge ourselves.[11]

Rarely did the bagatelles comment openly on politics or diplomacy. But when the story of Montresor at the gate of Paradise treated lightly the hot topic of religious tolerance, it became immediately the most popular and the most widely reprinted of the bagatelles.[12]

There once was an Officer, a man of means, named Montresor, who fell very ill. His Curate believing he was about to die, advised him to make his Peace with God in order to be received in Paradise. I have little Anxiety on that Score, said Montresor; for last night I had a Dream that left me very much at ease. What Dream did you have? said the good Priest. I was, says he, at the Gate of Paradise, with a Crowd of People who wanted to enter. And Saint Peter would ask each one what Religion he was.

One replied, I am a Roman Catholic. Good, Saint Peter said; Enter and take your Place among the Catholics. Another said he was of the Anglican Church. Very well, said Saint Peter, enter and take a Place among the Anglicans. Another said he was a Quaker. Enter, said Saint Peter, and take a Place among the Quakers.

At last he asked me of what Religion I was. Alas! I replied, unhappily poor Jacques Montresor has none. That's too bad, says the Saint—I do not know where to put you; but enter anyway and find a Place wherever you can.[13]

Franklin's more humorous bagatelles took the private-joke style of the *Craven Street Gazette,* in which Franklin played the role of straight man, as in the often reproduced conversation with the gout or in this less well-known whimsical address of his flies to Madame Helvétius.

The Flies in the Apartments of Monsieur F—n request permission to present their Respects to Madame H—s, & to express in their finest Language their Gratitude for the Protection that she has been kind enough to provide for them,

Bizz izzzz ouizz a ouizzzz izzzzzzzz, &c.

We have dwelt for a long time under the hospitable Roof of the said good Man F—n. He has given us free Lodging; we have also eaten & drunk all Year round at his Expense without Cost to us. Frequently when his Friends and he have emptied a Bowl of Punch, he has left a Quantity sufficient to intoxicate a hundred of us Flies. We have drunk it freely, & after that we have made our Sallies, our Circles & our Cotillions very prettily through the Air of his Chamber, & have gaily consummated our little Loves under his Nose. Briefly, we should have been the happiest People in the World, if he had not permitted to remain atop his Wainscoting a Number of our confirmed Enemies, who there spread their Nets to catch us, & piteously tear us to pieces. People with Dispositions both subtle and ferocious, abominable Combination! You, most excellent Woman, had the Benevolence to command that these Assassins be swept away with all their Lairs & Snares; & your Orders (as they always ought to be) were executed immediately. Since that Time we live happily, & enjoy the Beneficence of the aforesaid good Man Franklin unvexed.

Only One Thing remains to assure the Permanence of our Good Fortune; permit us to say,

Bizz izzzz ouizzzz izzzzzzzz, &c.

It is to see the two of you form a single Household.[14]

Franklin's familiar letters, though less widely circulated than the bagatelles, offered more room for exuberant humor, as in Franklin's letter on the beauties of wine, which fused whimsical fancy and scientific observation. He was responding to a drinking song by his friend Abbé André Morellet that claimed Americans rebelled because the British prohibited importing fine wine.

In vino veritas, says the wise man—*Truth is in wine.* Before the days of Noah, then, men, having nothing but water to drink, could not discover the truth. Thus they went astray, became abominably wicked, and were justly exterminated by *water,* which they loved to drink.

The good man Noah, seeing that through this pernicious beverage all his contemporaries had perished, took it in aversion; and to quench his thirst God created the vine, and revealed to him the means of converting its fruit into wine. By means of this liquor he discovered numberless important truths; so that ever since his time the word *to divine* has been in common use, signifying originally, *to discover by means of* **WINE.** Thus the patriarch Joseph took upon himself to *divine* by means of a cup or glass of **WINE** a liquor which obtained this name to show that it was not of human but *divine* invention . . .; nay, since that time, all things of peculiar excellence, even the Deities themselves, have been called *Divine* or *Divin*ities.

We hear of the conversion of water into wine at the marriage in Cana as of a miracle. . . . It is true that God has also instructed man to reduce wine into water. But into what sort of water?—*Water of Life* [i.e., eau-de-vie, or brandy]. And this, that man may be able upon occasion to perform the miracle of Cana, and convert common water into that excellent species of wine which we call *punch.*

My Christian brother, be kind and benevolent like God, and do not spoil his good work. He made wine to gladden the heart of man; do not, therefore, when at table you see your neighbor pour wine into his glass, be eager to mingle water with it. Why would you drown *truth?* . . . Do not, then, offer water, except to children;

'tis a mistaken piece of politeness, and often very inconvenient. I give you this hint as a man of the world; and I will finish as I began, like a good Christian, in making a religious observation of high importance, taken from the Holy Scriptures. I mean that the apostle Paul counselled Timothy very seriously to put wine into his water for the sake of his health; but that not one of the apostles or holy fathers ever recommended *putting water to wine.*

B. Franklin

P.S. To confirm still more your piety and gratitude to Divine Providence, reflect upon the situation which it has given to the *elbow.* You see in animals, who are intended to drink the waters that flow upon the earth, that if they have long legs, they have also a long neck, so that they can get at their drink without kneeling down. But man, who was destined to drink wine, is framed in a manner that he may raise the glass to his mouth. If the elbow had been placed nearer the hand, the part in advance would have been too short to bring the glass up to the mouth; and if it had been nearer the shoulder, that part would have been so long that when it attempted to carry the wine to the mouth it would have overshot the mark, and gone beyond the head; thus, either way, we should have been in the case of Tantalus. But from the actual situation of the elbow, we are enabled to drink at our ease, the glass going directly to the mouth. Let us, then, with glass in hand, adore this benevolent wisdom—let us adore and drink![15]

As a function of his diplomatic mission Franklin also produced satiric propaganda of the highest order. He contributed to the stream of protests flowing across France and the Low Countries aimed at German princes who supplied soldiers to fight in America. Worst was the Landgrave of Hesse-Cassel, Frederick the Second (not to be confused with Frederick the Great). The Landgrave contracted with Britain for 16,992 Hessians at $60 a head, dead or alive, with three wounded Hessians counting as one killed.[16]

The Landgrave justified the business as his people's only source of revenue.[17] Indeed, after the war, with profits of about $18,000,000, he employed two thousand men over fourteen years in building a Versailles-style palace as a vacation home.[18]

Franklin could see a comic side when the most powerful German ruler, Frederick the Great, reproved the Landgrave and others "by obliging them to pay him the same Toll per Head for the Men they drive thro' his Dominions, as used to be paid him for their *Cattle,* because they were sold as such."[19] After Washington's raid on Trenton killed seventeen Hessians and wounded seventy-eight, Franklin circulated a fictional letter from "Count de Schaumbergh to the Baron Hohendorf, Commanding the Hessian Troops in America"—another sketch of a mind adrift with no moral compass, the mechanical operation of the spirit.

As was his practice with propaganda, Franklin imitated a model well known to the public, in this instance Swift's "Modest Proposal" for easing Ireland's poverty by raising children for meat. Franklin's Count, like Swift's economist, plays with statistics that compound his absurdity. Swift modulates his irony with reasonable alternatives to the economist's plan. Franklin's unrelenting irony leaves the Count an unredeemed moral monster.

Rome, 18 February 1777

Monsieur le Baron:—

On my return from Naples, I received at Rome your Letter of the 27th December of last year. I have learned with unspeakable Pleasure the Courage our Troops exhibited at Trenton, and you cannot imagine my Joy on being told that of the 1,950 Hessians engaged in the Fight, but 345 escaped. There were just 1,605 Men killed, and I cannot sufficiently commend your Prudence in sending an exact List of the Dead to my Minister in London. This Precaution was the more necessary, as the Report sent to the English Ministry does not give but 1,455 Dead. This would make 483,450 Florins instead of the 643,500 which I am entitled to demand under our Convention. You will comprehend the Prejudice which such an Error would work in my Finances, and I do not doubt you will take the necessary Pains to prove that Lord North's List is false and yours correct.

The Court of London objects that there were a hundred Wounded who ought not to be included in the List, nor paid for as Dead; but I trust you will not overlook my Instructions to you on quitting Cassel, and that you will not have tried by Human Succor to recall to Life the Unfortunates whose Days could not be lengthened but by the Loss of a Leg or an Arm. That would be making them a pernicious Present, and I am sure they would rather die than live in a Condition no longer fit for my Service. I do not mean by this that you should assassinate them; we should be Humane, my dear Baron, but you may insinuate to the Surgeons with entire Propriety that a crippled Man is a reproach to their Profession, and that there is no wiser Course than to let every one of them die when he ceases to be fit to fight.

I am about to send to you some new Recruits. Don't economize them. Remember Glory before all Things. Glory is true Wealth. There is nothing degrades the Soldier like the Love of Money. He must care only for Honor and Reputation, but this Reputation must be acquired in the Midst of Dangers. A Battle gained without costing the Conqueror any Blood is an inglorious Success, while the Conquered cover themselves with Glory by perishing with their Arms in their Hands. Do you remember that of the 300 Lacedarmonians who defended the Defile of Thermopylae, not One returned? How happy should I be could I say the Same of my brave Hessians!

It is true that their King, Leonidas, perished with them: but Things have changed, and it is no longer the Custom for Princes of the Empire to go and fight in America for a Cause with which they have no Concern. And besides, to whom should they pay the thirty Guineas per Man if I did not stay in Europe to receive them? Then, it is necessary also that I be ready to send Recruits to replace the Men you lose. For this purpose I must return to Hesse. It is true, grown Men are becoming scarce there, but I will send you Boys. Besides, the scarcer the Commodity, the higher the Price.

I am assured that the Women and little Girls have begun to till our Lands, and they get on not badly.

You did right to send back to Europe that Dr. Crumerus who was so successful in curing Dysentery. Don't bother with a Man who is subject to Looseness of the Bowels. That Disease makes bad Soldiers. One Coward will do more Mischief in an Engagement than ten brave Men will do Good. Better that they burst in their Barracks than fly in a Battle, and tarnish the Glory of our Arms. Besides, you know that they pay me as Killed for all who die from Disease, and I don't get a Farthing for Runaways.

My Trip to Italy, which has cost me enormously, makes it desirable that there should be a great Mortality among them. You will therefore promise Promotion to all who expose themselves; you will exhort them to seek Glory in the midst of Dangers; you will say to Major Maundorff that I am not at all content with his Saving the 345 Men who escaped the Massacre at Trenton. Through the whole Campaign he has not had ten Men killed in consequence of his Orders. Finally, let it be your principal Object to prolong the War and avoid a decisive Engagement on either Side, for I have made Arrangements for a grand Italian Opera, and I do not wish to be obliged to give it up. Meantime I pray God, my dear Baron de Hohendorf, to have you in his holy and gracious Keeping.[20]

Franklin pushed the limits of this sort of irony when from his press at Passy he issued a broadside imitating a supplement to the Boston *Independent Chronicle* for 12 March 1782. The sheet, complete with authentic-looking advertisements, featured a bogus letter from the fictional Samuel Gerrish enclosing an intercepted invoice for eight large packages sent by the fictional James Craufurd to the actual military governor of Canada, General Frederick Haldimand. Gerrish counted 1,062 scalps collected on America's western frontier and sent as gifts to the British by friendly Seneca chiefs.

Franklin had witnessed effects of two earlier massacres. In 1763, Scotch-Irish frontiersmen, the Paxson Boys, angered by hostile raiders, took revenge on neighboring Moravian Indians. In

1755, while building forts on the frontier, Franklin found that hostile Indians had completely gutted the Moravian village of Gnadenhütten. Now in the same village in February 1782, frontiersmen massacred Moravian Indians—33 men and boys along with 36 women and girls—in retaliation for raids by hostile Indians.

He knew that frontiersmen were culpable. He should have known that General Haldimand had earlier rejected a plan to unleash Britain's Indian allies.[21] Yet he reverted to 1779 unfounded propaganda by George Rogers Clark who had dubbed British General Henry Hamilton of Detroit "the Famous Hair Buyer."[22] Thus Franklin shifted blame to Hamilton's allies and to their royal master: "It is he who has furnished the Savages with Hatchets and Scalping Knives, and engages them to fall upon our defenceless Farmers and murder them with their Wives and Children, paying for their Scalps, of which the account kept in America already amounts, as I have heard, to near two Thousand!"[23]

The report of fictional atrocities was palpable propaganda. Franklin confided to John Adams that he had some doubts of its "Veracity" but none of its "Substance. . . . These being *substantial* Truths the Form is to be considered as Paper and Packthread."[24] To enhance the newspaper's verisimilitude, he filled out the sheet with five realistic-looking advertisements. The remainder consisted of a letter by Samuel Gerrish enclosing a letter from the New York frontier to General Haldimand, itself enclosing an invoice of scalps, along with a mock speech as from Seneca chiefs. Gerrish's letter concludes with mordant humor that finally undercuts the clinical details.

Extract of a Letter from Capt. Gerrish, of the New-England Militia, dated Albany, March 7.

The Peltry taken in the Expedition *[See the Account of the Expedition to Oswegatchie on the River St. Laurence, in our Paper of the 1st Instant.]* will as you see amount to a good deal of Money. The Possession of this Booty at first gave us Pleasure; but we were struck with Horror to find among the Packages, 8 large ones containing S C A L P S of our unhappy Country-folks, taken in the three last Years by the Senneka Indians from the Inhabitants of the Frontiers of New-York, New-Jersey, Pennsylvania, and Virginia, and sent by them as a Present to Col. Haldimand, Governor of Canada, in order to be by him transmitted to England. They were accompanied by the following curious Letter to that Gentleman.

May it please your Excellency.
Teoga, Jan. 3d, 1782.

At the Request of the Senneka Chiefs I send herewith to your Excellency, under the Care of James Boyd, eight Packs of Scalps, cured, dried, hooped and painted, with all the Indian triumphal Marks, of which the following is Invoice and Explanation.

No. 1. Containing 43 Scalps of Congress Soldiers killed in different Skirmishes; these are stretched on black Hoops, 4 Inches diameter; the inside of the Skin painted red, with a small black Spot to note their being killed with Bullets. Also 62 of Farmers, killed in their Houses; the Hoops red; the Skin painted brown, and marked with a Hoe; a black Circle all round, to denote their being surprised in the Night; and a black Hatchet in the Middle, signifying their being killed with that Weapon.

No. 2. Containing 98 of Farmers killed in their Houses; Hoops red; Figure of a Hoe, to mark their Profession; great white Circle and Sun to shew they were surprised in the Day-time; a little red Foot, to shew they stood upon their Defence, and died fighting for their Lives and Families.

No. 3. Containing 97 of Farmers; Hoops green, to shew they were killed in their Fields; a large white Circle with a little round Mark on it for the Sun, to shew that it was in the Day-time; black Bullet-mark on some, Hatchet on others.

No. 4. Containing 102 of Farmers, mixed of the several Marks above; only 18 marked with a little yellow Flame, to denote their being of Prisoners burnt alive, after being scalped, their Nails pulled out by the Roots, and other Torments: one of these latter supposed to be of a rebel Clergyman, his Band being fixed to the Hoop of his Scalp. Most of the Farmers appear by the Hair to have been young or middle-aged Men; there being but 67 very grey Heads among them all, which makes the Service more essential.

No. 5. Containing 88 Scalps of Women; Hair long, braided in the Indian Fashion, to shew they were Mothers; Hoops blue; Skin yellow Ground, with little red Tadpoles to represent, by way of Triumph, the Tears of Grief occasioned to their Relations; a black scalping Knife or Hatchet at the Bottom, to mark their being killed with those Instruments. 17 others, Hair very grey; black Hoops; plain brown Colour; no Mark but the short Club or Cassetete, to shew they were knocked down dead, or had their Brains beat out.

No. 6. Containing 193 Boys' Scalps, of various Ages; small green Hoops; whitish Ground on the Skin, with red Tears in the Middle, and black Bullet-marks, Knife, Hatchet, or Club, as their Deaths happened.

No. 7. Girls' Scalps, big and little; small yellow Hoops; white Ground; Tears; Hatchet, Club, scalping Knife, &c.

No. 8. This Package is a Mixture of all the Varieties abovemention'd, to the Number of 122; with a Box of Birch Bark, containing 29 little Infants' Scalps of various Sizes; small white Hoops; white Ground; no Tears; and only a little black Knife in the Middle, to shew they were ript out of their Mothers' Bellies.

With these Packs, the Chiefs send to your Excellency the following Speech, delivered by Conejogatchie in Council, interpreted by the elder Moore, the Trader, and taken down by me in Writing.

Franklin's authentic imitation of passing out gifts—symbolic, ornamented belts—was based on his having attended or printed thirteen Indian treaties before the war.[25]

Father,

We send you herewith many Scalps, that you may see we are not idle Friends.

A blue Belt.

Father,

We wish you to send these Scalps over the Water to the great King, that he may regard them and be refreshed; and that he may see our faithfulness in destroying his Enemies, and be convinced that his Presents have not been made to ungrateful People.

A blue and white Belt with red Tassels.

Father,

Attend to what I am now going to say: it is a Matter of much Weight. The great King's Enemies are many, and they grow fast in Number. They were formerly like young Panthers: they could neither bite nor scratch: we could play with them safely: we feared nothing they could do to us. But now their Bodies are become big as the Elk, and strong as the Buffalo: they have also got great and sharp Claws. They have driven us out of our Country for taking Part in your Quarrel. We expect the great King will give us another Country, that our Children may live after us, and be his Friends and Children, as we are. Say this for us to the great King. To enforce it we give this Belt.

A great white Belt with blue Tassels.

Father,

We have only to say farther that your Traders exact more than ever for their Goods: and our Hunting is lessened by the War, so that we have fewer Skins to give for them. This ruins us. Think of some Remedy. We are poor: and you have Plenty of every Thing.

We know you will send us Powder and Guns, and Knives and Hatchets: but we also want Shirts and Blankets.

A little white Belt.

I do not doubt but that your Excellency will think it proper to give some farther Encouragement to those honest People. The high Prices they complain of, are the necessary Effect of the War. Whatever Presents may be sent for them through my Hands, shall be distributed with Prudence and Fidelity. I have the Honour of being

Your Excellency's most obedient
And most humble Servant,
James Craufurd.

It was at first proposed to bury these Scalps: but Lieutenant Fitzgerald, who you know has got Leave of Absence to go for Ireland on his private Affairs, said he thought it better they should proceed to their Destination; and if they were given to him, he would undertake to carry them to England, and hang them all up in some dark Night on the Trees in St. James's Park, where they could be seen from the King and Queen's Palaces in the Morning; for that the Sight of them might perhaps strike Muley Ishmael (as he called him) with some Compunction of Conscience.

The pun, "Muley Ishmael," skewers George III by confusing him with the bloodthirsty Moroccan ruler Mawlay Ismail (1672–1727), who used an army of black sub-Saharan slaves to subdue his own people.

They were accordingly delivered to Fitz, and he has brought them safe hither. To-morrow they go with his Baggage in a Waggon for Boston, and will probably be there in a few Days after this letter.

I am, &c.
Samuel Gerrish.

Boston, March 20.

Monday last arrived here Lieutenant Fitzgerald above-mentioned, and Yesterday the Waggon with the Scalps. Thousands of People are flocking to see them this Morning, and all Mouths are full of Execrations. Fixing them to the Trees is not approved. It is now proposed to make them up in decent little Packets, seal and direct them; one to the King, containing a Sample of every Sort for his Museum; one to the Queen, with some of Women and little Children: the Rest to be distributed among both Houses of Parliament; a double Quantity to the Bishops.[26]

8

Comic Release

1783–1785

The war ended with a preliminary agreement, 20 January 1783, but Franklin had little peace. Since the summer of 1781, worn out by the ills of old age and sick of bickering with members of his own delegation, especially John Adams, he had been petitioning Congress to relieve him. Congressmen influenced by Adams and former commissioner Arthur Lee argued that Franklin's popularity in France proved that he was a covert French agent. They wished to recall him, but an opposite and equal faction wished to recall Adams. The impasse dissolved in mid-March 1785, when they named Adams ambassador to Britain and finally granted Franklin permission to go home. Until that time, although immobilized by gout, kidney stones, and prostatitis, he served valiantly as the United States ambassador, "being oblig'd to perform all the Functions of Consul, Judge of Admiralty, Merchant, Banker, &c. &c."[1] He prepared pamphlets about America and Americans and, as a scientist, spent five months working on an eighty-page report for the king of France on mesmerism. He routinely attended cultural and scientific meetings and kept up correspondence with other scientists worldwide, including at least a hundred letters from Jan Ingenhouse, Dutch physician to Empress Maria Theresa of Austria.[2]

With no further need to attack the British government,

Franklin's satirical writings adopted the gentler tone of the bagatelles. He reassumed Silence Dogood's role as cultural gadfly. Given his interest in science, he satirized the virtuosi as dilettantes who debased and thereby devalued scientific method. Their eccentric experimentation led to the mechanical operation of the spirit, as in the case of the virtuoso angered when interrupted by a call to dinner: "What have you for Dinner?"—"Ham and Chickens."—"Ham! and must I break the Chain of my Thoughts, to go down and gnaw a Morsel of a damn'd Hogs Arse? I shall dine tomorrow."[3]

Franklin's masterpiece of antivirtuoso satire is his classic proposal for daylight savings, which he composed with mature understanding of his model but without the savagery of Swift's "Modest Proposal." Swift's projector proposed to solve impoverished Ireland's hunger by consuming her children. But in ridiculing the horrible plan, Swift offered alternatives, as does Franklin in his daylight savings proposal. Franklin's exuberant economist even garbled the arithmetic, as Swift's projector had done in calculating the cost-effective number of breeders.

As a parody of the typical virtuoso technical report, Franklin wrote it as a sort of private joke to the *Journal de Paris.* The newspaper, founded by his friend, chemist Antoine Alexis Cadet de Vaux, was edited by a closer friend, Jacques Barbeu-Dubourg, who, having translated Franklin's science into French, perhaps translated this piece too. Franklin's timely satire appeared on 26 April 1784, coinciding with wide popular acclaim for a new invention by two other friends, merchant Ambroise Lange and pharmacist Antoine Quinquet. Their smokeless oil lamp gave light ten times brighter than ever before. (Alas, before the year was out, Quinquet confessed in the *Journal de Paris* that they had copied the idea from still another friend, Ami Argand, whose name the lamp still bears.[4]) By opening with a reference to their invention, Franklin signified that because the new lamps dimmed the future of candles, the feckless economist's elaborate proposal was obsolescent and unnecessary. His proof seemed so ridiculous as to blind casual readers to the plan's actual benefits, which were not fully realized until the twentieth century.

To the Authors of the Journal of Paris

Messieurs,

You often entertain us with accounts of new discoveries. Permit me to communicate to the public, through your paper, one that has been lately made by myself, and which I conceive may be of great utility.

I was the other evening in a grand company, where the new lamp of Messrs. Quinquet and Lange was introduced, and much admired for its splendor; but a general enquiry was made, whether the oil it consumed was not in proportion to the light it afforded, in which case there would be no saving in the use of it. No one present could satisfy us in this point, which all agreed ought to be known, it being a very desirable thing to lessen, if possible, the expense of lighting our apartments, when every other article of family expense was so much augmented.

I was much pleased to see this general concern for economy; for I love economy exceedingly.

I went home, and to bed, three or four hours after midnight, with my head full of the subject. An accidental sudden noise waked me about six in the morning, when I was surprised to find my room filled with light, and I imagined at first, that a number of those lamps had been brought into it; but rubbing my eyes I perceived the light came in at the windows. I got up and looked out to see what might be the occasion of it, when I saw the sun just rising above the horizon, from whence he poured his rays plentifully into my chamber, my domestic having negligently omitted the preceding night to close the shutters.

I looked at my watch, which goes very well, and found that it was but six o'clock; and still thinking it something extraordinary that the sun should rise so early, I looked into the almanack, where I found it to be the hour given for his rising on that day. I looked forward, too, and found he was to rise still earlier every day till towards the end of June; and that at no time in the year he retarded his rising so long as till eight o'clock. Your readers, who with me have never seen any signs of sunshine before noon, and seldom regard the astronomical part of the almanack, will be as much astonished as I was, when they hear of his rising so early; and especially when I assure them that he gives light as soon as he rises; I am convinced of this. I am certain of my fact. One cannot be more certain of any fact. I saw it with my own eyes. And having repeated this observation the three following mornings, I found always precisely the same result.

Yet so it happens, that when I speak of this discovery to others, I can easily perceive by their countenances, though they forbear expressing it in words, that they do not quite believe me. One indeed, who is a learned natural philosopher [scientist], has assured me that I must certainly be mistaken as to the circumstance of the light coming into my room; for it being well known, as he says, that there could be no light abroad at that hour, it follows that none could enter from without; and that of consequence, my windows being accidentally left open, instead of letting in the light, had only served to let out the darkness; and he used many ingenious arguments to shew me how I might by that means have been deceived. I own that he puzzled me a little, but he did not satisfy me; and the subsequent observations I made, as abovementioned, confirmed me in my first opinion.

This event has given rise in my mind to several serious and important reflections. I considered that if I had not been awakened so early that morning, I should have slept six hours longer by the light of the sun, and in exchange have lived six hours the following night by candle light; and the latter being a much more expensive light than the former, my love of economy induced me to muster up what little arithmetic I was master of, and to make some calculations, which I shall give you, after observing that utility is, in my opinion, the test of value in matters of invention, and that a discovery which can be applied to no use, or is not good for something, is good for nothing.

I took for the basis of my calculation the supposition that there are 100,000 families in Paris, and that these families consume in the night half a pound of bougies, or candles, per hour. I think this a moderate allowance, taking one family with another; for though I believe some consume less, I know that many consume a great deal more. Then estimating seven hours per day, as the medium quantity between the time of the sun's rising and ours, he rising during the six following months from six to eight hours before noon—and there being seven hours of course per night in which we burn candles, the account will stand thus:

In the six months between the 20th of March and the 20th of September, there are

Nights,—	183
Hours of each night in which we burn candles,—	7
Multiplication gives us for the total number of hours,—	1,281
These 1281 hours, multiplied by 100,000, the number of families, give—	128,100,000
One hundred twenty-eight millions and one hundred thousand hours, spent at Paris by candle-light, which at half a pound of wax and tallow per hour, gives the weight of—	64,050,000
Sixty-four millions and fifty thousand of pounds, which, estimating the whole at the medium price of thirty sols the pound, makes the sum of ninety-six millions and seventy-five thousand livres tournois—	96,075,000

An immense sum! that the city of Paris might save every year, by the economy of using sun-shine instead of candles.

If it should be said that people are apt to be obstinately attached to old customs, and that it will be difficult to induce them to rise before noon, consequently my discovery can be of but little use; I answer, *nil desperandum [no problem!]*. I believe all who have common sense, as soon as they have learnt from this paper that it is day-light when the sun rises, will contrive to rise with him;

and, to compel the rest, I would propose the following regulations:

First. Let a tax be laid of a louis per window, on every window that is provided with shutters to keep out the light of the sun.

Second. Let the same salutary operation of police be made use of, to prevent our burning candles that inclined us last winter to be more economical in burning wood; that is, let guards be placed in the shops of all the wax and tallow chandlers, and no family be permitted to be supplied with more than one pound of candles per week.

Third. Let guards also be posted to stop all the coaches, &c. that would pass the streets after sun-set, except those of physicians, surgeons, and midwives.

Fourth. Every morning, as soon as the sun rises, let all the bells in every church be set ringing; and if that is not sufficient, let cannon be fired in every street, to wake the sluggards effectually, and to make them open their eyes to see their true interest.

All the difficulty will be in the first two or three days; after which the reformation will be as natural and easy, as the present irregularity: for, *ce n'est que le premier pas qui coûte [the first step is hardest].* Oblige a man to rise at four in the morning, and it is more than probable he shall go willingly to bed at eight in the evening; and having had eight hours sleep, he will rise more willingly at four in the morning following.

But this sum of ninety-six millions and seventy-five thousand livres, is not the whole of what may be saved by my economical project. You may observe, that I have calculated upon only one-half of the year, and much may be saved in the other, though the days are shorter. Besides, the immense stock of wax and tallow left unconsumed during the summer, will probably make candles much cheaper for the ensuing winter, and continue cheaper as long as the proposed reformation shall be supported.

For the great benefit of this discovery, thus freely communicated and bestowed by me on the public, I demand neither place, pension, exclusive privilege, or any other reward whatever. I expect only to have the honour of it. And yet I know there are little envious minds who will, as usual, deny me this, and say that my invention was known to the ancients, and perhaps they may bring passages out of old books in proof of it. I will not dispute with these people that the ancients might know the sun would rise at certain hours; they possibly had, as we have, almanacks that predicted it; but it does not follow from thence, that they knew he gave light as soon as he rose. This is what I claim as my discovery. If the ancients knew it, it must have been long since forgotten, for it certainly was unknown to the moderns, at least to the Parisians, which to prove, I need use but one simple argument. They are as well-instructed, judicious, and prudent a people as exist any where in the world, all professing like myself to be lovers of economy; and from the many heavy taxes required from them by the necessities of the state, have surely an abundant reason to be economical. I say it is impossible that so sensible a people, under such circumstances, should have lived so long by the smoaky unwholesome and enormously expensive light of candles, if they had really known that they might have had as much pure light of the sun for nothing. I am, &c.

An ABONNE [A Subscriber][5]

Au courant on experiments in ballooning, Franklin teased Joseph Priestley, the discoverer of oxygen, with a timely comment on the public debate in 1783 over the merits of their mutual friend J. A. C. Charles's balloon, which lifted with hydrogen, versus the Montgolfiers' balloon, which used hot air.[6]

Gentlemen—

It is said that chemists are making every effort to discover an air which is lighter and more expansive than the inflammable gas now used to fill Aerostats (the name given to balloons by our learned academies). It is singular, indeed, that men as enlightened as these of our age are constantly making researches in art, for that which nature is all the time offering to everybody, and that a fool like me should be the first to suggest the application of it.

I shall not demand any recompense from Government nor any exclusive privilege. If you wish to fill your balloons with a material ten times lighter than inflammable air, you will find it in great quantity in the Promises of Lovers and Courtiers; in the sighs of widowers, in the good resolutions made in a storm at sea, and in sickness on land, and above all, in the compliments contained in Letters of Recommendation.

I am &c. Une Abonnée.[7]

It would surprise no one if this comment on gas inspired Franklin's classic burlesque of scientific papers such as he himself often wrote. Impersonating a practicing virtuoso, he responded to the actual contest sponsored by Brussels' Royal Academy of Science and Belles Letters. The practicing virtuoso opens by repeating the Academy's question published 19 May 1780 (later withdrawn as altogether impossible). Franklin could have found additional inspiration in one of the Academy's actual studies that speculated on the impact of meteorology on personal hygeine.[8] In any case, he enriched the fun by parodying the style of his own reports. He limited the six-page pamphlet to his friends' eyes only.[9]

To the Royal Academy of——

Gentlemen,

I have perused your late mathematical Prize Question, proposed in lieu of one in Natural Philosophy, for the ensuing year, viz.

[Within the given single figure, inscribe the greatest number of the smaller figure, also given.] I was glad to find by these following Words, *[The Academy has judged that the solution, by expanding the frontiers of knowledge, will not be without* ***Utility****,]* that you esteem *Utility* an essential Point in your Enquiries, which has not always been the case with all Academies; and I conclude therefore that you have given this Question instead of a philosophical [abstract],

or as the Learned express it, a physical one [applied], because you could not at the time think of a physical one that promis'd greater *Utility*.

Permit me then humbly to propose one of that sort for your consideration, and through you, if you approve it, for the serious Enquiry of learned Physicians, Chemists, &c. of this enlightened Age.

It is universally well known, That in digesting our common Food, there is created or produced in the Bowels of human Créatures, a great Quantity of Wind.

That the permitting this Air to escape and mix with the Atmosphere, is usually offensive to the Company, from the fetid Smell that accompanies it.

That all well-bred People therefore, to avoid giving such Offence, forcibly restrain the Efforts of Nature to discharge that Wind.

That so retain'd contrary to Nature, it not only gives frequently great present Pain, but occasions future Diseases, such as habitual Cholics, Ruptures, Tympanies, &c. often destructive of the Constitution, & sometimes of Life itself.

Were it not for the odiously offensive Smell accompanying such Escapes, polite People would probably be under no more Restraint in discharging such Wind in Company, than they are in spitting, or in blowing their Noses.

My Prize Question therefore should be, *To discover some Drug wholesome & not disagreable, to be mix'd with our common Food, or Sauces, that shall render the natural Discharges of Wind from our Bodies, not only inoffensive, but agreable as Perfumes.*

That this is not a chimerical Project, and altogether impossible, may appear from these Considerations. That we already have some Knowledge of Means capable of *Varying* that Smell. He that dines on stale Flesh, especially with much Addition of Onions, shall be able to afford a Stink that no Company can tolerate; while he that has lived for some Time on Vegetables only, shall have that Breath so pure as to be insensible to the most delicate Noses; and if he can manage so as to avoid the Report, he may any where give Vent to his Griefs, unnoticed. But as there are many to whom an entire Vegetable Diet would be inconvenient, and as a little Quick-Lime thrown into a Jakes will correct the amazing Quantity of fetid Air arising from the vast Mass of putrid Matter contain'd in such Places, and render it rather pleasing to the Smell, who knows but that a little Powder of Lime (or some other thing equivalent) taken in our Food, or perhaps a Glass of Limewater drank at Dinner, may have the same Effect on the Air produc'd in and issuing from our Bowels? This is worth the Experiment.

Certain it is also that we have the Power of changing by slight Means the Smell of another Discharge, that of our Water. A few Stems of Asparagus eaten, shall give our Urine a disagreable Odour; and a Pill of Turpentine no bigger than a Pea, shall bestow on it the pleasing Smell of Violets. And why should it be thought more impossible in Nature, to find Means of making a Perfume of our *Wind* than of our *Water?*

For the Encouragement of this Enquiry,(from the immortal Honour to be reasonably expected by the Inventor) let it be considered of how small Importance to Mankind, or to how small a Part of Mankind have been useful those Discoveries in Science that have heretofore made Philosophers famous. Are there twenty Men in Europe at this Day, the happier, or even the easier, for any knowledge they have pick'd out of Aristotle? What comfort can the Vortices of Descartes give to a Man who has Whirlwinds in his Bowels! The Knowledge of Newton's mutual *Attraction* of the Particles of Matter, can it afford Ease to him who is rack'd by their mutual *Repulsion,* and the cruel Distensions it occasions? The Pleasure arising to a few Philosophers, from seeing, a few Times in their Life, the Threads of Light untwisted, and separated by the Newtonian Prism into seven Colours, can it be compared with the Ease and Comfort every Man living might feel seven times a Day, by discharging freely the Wind from his Bowels? Especially if it be converted into a Perfume: For the Pleasures of one Sense being little inferior to those of another, instead of pleasing the *Sight* he might delight the *Smell* of those about him, & make Numbers happy, which to a benevolent Mind must afford infinite Satisfaction. The generous Soul who now endeavours to find out whether the Friends he entertains like best Claret or Burgundy, Champagne or Madeira, would then enquire also whether they chose Musk or Lilly, Rose or Bergamot, and provide accordingly. And surely such a Liberty of *Ex-pressing* one's *Scent-iments,* and *pleasing one another,* is of infinitely more Importance to human Happiness than that Liberty of the *Press,* or *abusing one another,* which the English are so ready to fight & die for.—

In short, this Invention, if compleated, would be, as *Bacon* expresses it, *bringing Philosophy home to Mens Business and Bosoms.* And I cannot but conclude, that in Comparison therewith, for *universal* and *continual* UTILITY, the Science of the Philosophers abovementioned, even with the Addition, Gentlemen, of your "*Figure quelconque*" [given Figure] and the Figures inscrib'd in it, are, all together, scarcely worth a ***FART-HING.***[10]

Franklin himself had been fascinated by applied mathematics since the days when he drew magic squares and circles to ease the boredom of clerking in the Pennsylvania legislature. He humorously applied simple arithmetic to show the absurdity of a nobility founded on birth, such as proposed by the Society of the Cincinnati, a fraternity of American officers from the Revolution who would leave their membership as a legacy to heirs. Replying to daughter Sally's request for comment, Franklin simply pursued their premise to its logical absurdity.

A Man's Son, for instance, is but half of his Family, the other half belonging to the family of his Wife. His Son, too, marrying into another Family, his Share in the Grandson is but a fourth; in the Great Grandson, by the same Process, it is but an Eighth; in the next generation a Sixteenth; the next a Thirty-second; the next a Sixty-fourth; the next a hundred and Fifty-sixth; and the next a Five hundred and twelfth; thus in nine Generations, which will not require more than 300 years (no very great Antiquity for a Family), our present Chevalier of the Order of Cincinnatus's Share in the then existing Knight, will be but a 512th part; which, allowing the present certain Fidelity of American Wives to be insur'd down through all those Nine Generations, is so small a Consideration, that methinks no reasonable Man would hazard for the sake of it the disagreable Consequences of the Jealousy, Envy, and Ill will of his Countrymen. . . . One Thousand and Twenty-two Men and Women, contributors to the formation of one Knight. And, if we are to have a Thousand of these future knights, there must be now and hereafter existing One million and Twenty-two Thousand Fathers and Mothers, who are to contribute to their Production, unless a Part of the Number are employ'd in making more Knights than One. Let us strike off then the 22,000, on the Supposition of this double Employ, and then consider whether, after a reasonable Estimation of the Number of Rogues, and Fools, and Royalists and Scoundrels and Prostitutes, that are mix'd with, and help to make up necessarily their Million of Predecessors, Posterity will have much reason to boast of the noble Blood of the then existing Set of Chevaliers de Cincinnatus.[11]

Franklin respected the officers' gallantry but could not restrain laughing at their vanity with a typical apologue. He reminded his daughter, "You know every thing makes me recollect some Story," and he told of the gentleman who spent a fortune to erect a fine house and took great pride in showing it to visitors. One friend asked the meaning of a motto over the door that began with an overline above the initial O in *Omnia Vanitas* (all is vanity).

"What," says he, "is the Meaning of this OIA? It is a word I don't understand."

"I will tell you," said the gentleman: "I had a mind to have the Motto cut on a Piece of smooth Marble, but there was not room for it between the Ornaments, to be put in Characters large enough to be read. I therefore made use of a Contraction antiently very common in Latin Manuscripts, by which the *m's* and *n's* in Words are omitted, and the Omission noted by a little Dash above, which you may see there. . . ."

"O," says his Friend, "I now comprehend the Meaning of your Motto, it relates to your Edifice; and signifies that, if you have abridged your *Omnia,* you have, nevertheless, left your VANITAS legible at full length."[12]

As if by habit, Franklin relied on such humorous apologues to fortify his position or make a point more forcefully. As earlier he had shielded himself from office seekers with a universal letter of application, so to dam a flood of letters from prospective immigrants, he printed a serious twelve-page pamphlet, *Information to Those who Would Remove to America,* along with a companion pamphlet on American Indians.[13] To the manuscript of the former, he appended a note in a ridiculous dialect on how Americans view gentlemen of leisure.

They are pleas'd with the Observation of a Negro, and frequently mention it, that Boccarorra (meaning the Whiteman) make de Blackman workee, make de Horse workee, make de Ox workee, make ebery ting workee; only de Hog. He de Hog, no workee; he eat, he drink, he walk about, he go to sleep when he please, *he libb like a Gentleman.*[14]

In the pamphlet on Indians, *Remarks Concerning the Savages of North America,* Franklin resurrected as an apologue the Senecan creation myth he had published several years earlier in the *London Chronicle.* The dialogue captures the Native Americans' characteristic put-on of poker-faced gravitas as they matched creation myths with the missionary.

In the Beginning, our Fathers had only the Flesh of Animals to subsist on; and if their Hunting was unsuccessful, they were starving. Two of our young Hunters, having kill'd a Deer, made a Fire in the Woods to broil some Part of it. When they were about to satisfy their Hunger, they beheld a beautiful young Woman descend from the Clouds, and seat herself on that Hill, which you see yonder among the blue Mountains. They said to each other, it is a Spirit that has smelt our broiling Venison, and wishes to eat of it; let us offer some to her. They presented her with the Tongue;

she was pleas'd with the Taste of it, and said, "Your kindness shall be rewarded; come to this Place after thirteen Moons, and you shall find something that will be of great Benefit in nourishing you and your Children to the latest Generations." They did so, and to their Surprise, found Plants they had never seen before; but which, from that ancient time, have been constantly cultivated among us, to our great Advantage. Where her right Hand had touched the Ground, they found Maize; where her left hand had touch'd it, they found Kidney-Beans; and where her Backside had sat on it, they found Tobacco.[15]

Franklin applied his apologues as balm for American youths, Mason Locke "Parson" Weems and Edward Gant, after their applications for ordination had been rejected by the Archbishop of Canterbury. To console them, Franklin said the Archbishop had as little regard for souls as Lord Treasurer Edward Seymour had shown years earlier when James Blair sought a grant from the Queen for the College of William and Mary.

He oppos'd the Grant . . . he did not see the least Occasion for a College in Virginia. Blair represented to him, that its Intention was to educate and qualify young Men to be Ministers of the Gospel, much wanted there; and begged [Seymour] would consider, that the People of Virginia had souls to be saved, as well as the People of England. "Souls!" says he, *"damn your Souls. Make Tobacco!"*[16]

Franklin could console himself with mordant apologues even in private moments of darkest despair, as when, during the war, he compared inanimate works of nature to human nature: "The more I discover'd of the latter, the more I am disgusted with them." He was reflecting on the massive Anglo-French naval battle near Martinque and Dominica (12 April 1782), where the one-day engagement left at least 400 dead and 700 wounded.

In what Light we are viewed by superior Beings, may be gathered from a Piece of late West India News. . . . A young Angel of

Distinction being sent down to this World on some Business, for the first time, had an old Courier-Spirit assigned him as a Guide. They arriv'd over the Seas of Martinico in the middle of the long Day of obstinate Fight between the Fleets of [George] Rodney and [François] De Grasse. When, thro' the Clouds of Smoke, he saw the Fire of the Guns, the Decks covered with mangled Limbs, and Bodies dead or dying; the Ships sinking, burning, or blown into the Air; and the Quantity of Pain, Misery, and Destruction, the Crews yet alive were thus with so much Eagerness dealing round to one another; he turn'd angrily to his Guide, and said, You blundering Blockhead, you are ignorant of your Business; you undertook to conduct me to the Earth, and you have brought me into Hell!

No, Sir, says the Guide, I have made no mistake; this is really the Earth, and these are Men. Devils never treat one another in this cruel manner; they have more Sense, and more of what Men (vainly) call *Humanity*.[17]

Franklin found relief in humor recollected over sixty years. In January 1722, the *New-England Courant* had alluded to a Connecticut trader furious with his investment in onions: "The more they are cursed, the more they grow." Sixty-three years later, Franklin created an apologue to reassure his nephew Jonathan Williams about the London gossip that America faced financial disaster.

They are angry with us and hate us, and speak all manner of evil of us; but we flourish, notwithstanding. They put me in mind of a violent High Church Factor, resident some time in Boston, when I was a Boy. He had bought upon Speculation a Connecticut Cargo of Onions, which he flatter'd himself he might sell again to great Profit, but the Price fell, and they lay upon hand. He was heartily vex'd with his Bargain, especially when he observ'd they began to *grow* in the Store he had fill'd with them. He show'd them one Day to a Friend. "Here they are," says he, "and they are growing too! I damn 'em every day; but I think they are like the Prebyterians; the more I curse 'em, the more they grow."[18]

9

Revising Past and Future

1786–1790

Philadelphians met Franklin at the wharf on 14 September 1785 and paraded him home to Market Street "with acclamations of joy," the booming of cannon, and the pealing of bells. They elected him president of the Supreme Executive Council as Pennsylvania's hope for "reconciling all parties."[1] Gossips claimed that councilors humored him in the morning and waited for him to leave before they took care of business.[2] Records show that he presided at only one session in six.[3] The pain of his many ills could be eased only by laudanum, the household remedy made from opium. The comic muse was no substitute for opium, yet he continued to write humorous material for friends and for the local press.

Eighty-year-old Franklin found no relief from national service. As a delegate to the Federal Constitutional Convention of 1787, he was often too weak to speak, and others read his speeches for him. The records show few flashes of his apologues. During debates on the judiciary, he told "in a brief and entertaining manner" how Scotch judges were appointed by lawyers "who always selected the ablest of the profession in order to get rid of him, and share his practice among themselves."[4] Because proceedings were secret, newspapers provided epitomes of his familiar apologues. In reporting Franklin's famous appeal for compromise at the Convention (17 September), they published paraphrases where we would expect full-scale apologues. In that widely reported speech, as in his early practice, Franklin drew two anecdotes from sources known to his audience, the first by Richard Steele, and the second by Paris friend Madame La Freté.[5]

—Most men indeed, as well as most sects in religion, think themselves in possession of all truth, and that wherever others differ from them, it is so far errour. Steele, a Protestant, in a dedication, tells the Pope, that the only difference between our two churches, in their opinions of the certainty of their doctrine, is, the Romish church is infallible, and the church of England is *never in the wrong.*

—But though many private persons, think almost as highly of their own infallibility as that of their Sect—few express it so naturally as a certain French lady, who in a little dispute with her sister, said, I do not know how it happens, sister, but I meet with no body but myself that is always in the right.[6]

While the Convention was in session, Franklin organized a Society for Political Enquiry holding seminars at his home to study problems facing the innovative democratic republic. Among studies of long-range finance and urban problems, Franklin proposed a timely study of freedom of the press, a problem he had faced in earliest days on the *New-England Courant* and now encountered with renewed anxiety. During the intense state conventions being held to ratify the Constitution, the press replaced debate with invective, even calling Franklin an old fool.[7] From his sickbed, the weary veteran of newspaper wars of sixty years wrote to preserve Pennsylvania's unicameral system that he had proposed first to the Albany Congress in 1754 and later to the Continental Congress in 1776. He concocted an attack on bicameralism with a fable as sharp as the fables he had wielded against the British Parliament.

Has not the famous political Fable of the Snake, with two Heads and one Body, some useful Instruction contained in it? She was going to a Brook to drink, and in her Way was to pass thro' a Hedge, a Twig of which opposed her direct Course; one Head chose to go on the right Side of the Twig, the other on the left; so that time was spent in the Contest, and, before the Decision was completed, the poor Snake died with thirst.[8]

In earlier conflicts, Franklin had relied on his own pen against almanac competitors, religious zealots, greedy proprietors, power-mad parliaments, and unruly kings. Now, on 23 November 1787, he asked the Society for Political Enquiry to study the responsibility that came with a free press.[9] Another sign of his deep concern was a draft he did not publish complaining about the "Spirit of Rancour, Malice, and *Hatred*" in Philadelphia newspapers. Using actual quotations and a device of his earliest satires, he posed as a naive New Yorker who knows only what she reads in the newspapers. Besides being shocked by the partisan invective she quotes, she is puzzled by Philadelphians' attitude towards their public servants.

Witness a *"petty Fidler, Sycophant, and Scoundrel"* appointed Judge of the Admiralty; *"an old Woman and Fomenter of Sedition"* to be another of the Judges . . . with *"two Harpies"* the Comptroller and Naval Officers, to prey upon the Merchants and deprive them of their Property by Force of Arms, &c. I am inform'd also by these Papers, that your General Assembly, tho' the annual choice of the People, shows no regard to their Rights, but from sinister Views or Ignorance makes Laws in direct Violation of the Constitution . . . and finally, that your President [Franklin himself], the unanimous joint choice of the Council and Assembly, is *"an old Rogue,"* who gave his Assent to the federal Constitution merely to avoid refunding Money he had purloin'd from the United States.[10]

At a time when Congress refused to reimburse Franklin's expenses in France because of mistakes in his accounting,[11] having the press accuse him of embezzlement stung sharply. He fought back with the fervor of old in the *Federal Gazette* of 12 September

1789. In a paper probably prepared for the Society for Political Enquiry, he confronted the problem of an unrestrained press guaranteed by Pennsylvania's state constitution of 1776, the source of his antagonists' slogan, "The freedom of the press ought not to be restrained."[12]

Franklin entitled this final humorous parody, "An Account of the Supremest Court of Judicature in Pennsylvania, viz. The Court of the Press." His style parodied the legal jargon in September's congressional debates on the Judiciary Act and especially on the Bill of Rights. The senate had just defeated a motion to extend a blanket freedom to the press "in as ample a manner as hath at any time been secured by the common law."[13] As in Franklin's previous satires, he impersonates a virtuoso projector. The fail-safe plan in fact catalogs the actual practice of the press.

Power of this Court.

It may receive and promulgate accusations of all kinds against all persons and characters among the citizens of the state, and even against inferior courts, and may judge, sentence and condemn to infamy, not only private individuals, but public bodies, &c. with or without enquiry or hearing, *at the court's discretion.*

In whose favor or for whose emolument this court is established.

In favor of about one citizen in 500, who by education, or practice in scribbling, has acquired a tolerable stile as to grammar and construction so as to bear printing; or who is possessed of a press and a few types. This 500th part of the citizens have the privilege of accusing and abusing the other 499 parts, at their pleasure; or they may hire out their pens and press to others for that purpose.

Practice of the Court.

It is not governed by any of the rules of common courts of law. The accused is allowed no grand jury to judge of the truth of the accusation before it is publicly made . . . The proceedings are also sometimes so rapid, that an honest good citizen may find himself suddenly and unexpectedly accused, and in the same morning judged and condemned, and sentence pronounced against him, That he is a *rogue* and a *villain.* Yet if an officer of this court receives the slightest check for misconduct in this his office, he claims immediately the rights of a free citizen by the constitution, and demands to know his accuser, to confront the witnesses, and to have a fair trial by a jury of his peers.

The foundation of its authority.

It is said to be founded on an article in the state-constitution, which established *the liberty of the Press.* A liberty which every Pennsylvanian would fight and die for: Though few of us, I believe, have distinct ideas of its nature and extent. It seems indeed somewhat like the *liberty* of the *press* that felons have by the common law of England before conviction, that is, to be either *pressed* to death or hanged. If by the *liberty of the Press* were understood merely the liberty of discussing the propriety of public measures and political opinions, let us have as much of it as you please; But if it means the liberty of affronting, calumniating and defaming one another, I, for my part, own myself willing to part with my share of it, whenever our legislators shall please so to alter the law and shall chearfully consent to exchange my *liberty* of abusing others for the *privilege* of not being abused myself.

By whom this court is commissioned or constituted . . .

Any man who can procure pen, ink, and paper, with a press, a few types, and a huge pair of BLACKING balls, may commissionate himself: And his court is immediately established in the plenary possession and exercise of its rights. For if you make the least complaint of the *judge's* conduct, he daubs his blacking balls in your face wherever he meets you; and besides tearing your private character to slitters, marks you out for the odium of the public, as an *enemy to the liberty of the Press. . . .*

Of the checks proper to be established against the abuse of power in those courts.

Hitherto there are none. But since so much has been written and published on the federal constitution, and the necessity of checks in all other parts of good government has been so clearly and learnedly explained, I find myself so far enlightened as to suspect some check may be proper in this part also; but I have been at a loss to imagine any that may not be construed an infringement of the sacred *liberty of the Press.* At length however I think I have found one, that instead of diminishing general liberty, shall augment it; which is, by restoring to the people a species of liberty of which they have been deprived by our laws, I mean the *liberty of the Cudgel.*—In the rude state of society, prior to the existence of laws, if one man gave another ill language, the affronted person might return it by a box on the ear; and if repeated, by a good drubbing; and this without offending against any law; but now the right of making such returns is denied, and they are punished as breaches of the peace; while the right of abusing seems to remain in full force: the laws made against it being rendered ineffectual by the *liberty of the Press.*

My proposal then is, to leave the liberty of the Press untouched, to be exercised in its full extent, force and vigour, but to permit the *liberty of the Cudgel* to go with it *pari passu* [on equal terms]. Thus my fellow citizens, if an impudent writer attacks your reputation, dearer to you perhaps than your life, and puts his name to the charge, you may go to him as openly and break his head. If he conceals himself behind the printer, and you can nevertheless discover who he is, you may in like manner way-lay him in the night, attack him behind, and give him a good drubbing. If your adversary hires better writers than himself to abuse you the more effectually, you may hire brawny porters, stronger than yourself, to assist you in giving him a more effectual drubbing.—Thus far goes my project, as to *private* resentment and retribution. But if the public should ever happen to be affronted, *as it ought to be* with the conduct of such writers, I would not advise proceeding immediately to these extremities; but that we should in moderation content ourselves with tarring and feathering, and tossing them in a blanket.

If, however, it should be thought that this proposal of mine may disturb the public peace, I would then humbly recommend to our legislators to take up the consideration of both liberties, that of the Press, and that of the Cudgel, and by an explicit law mark their extent and limits; and at the same time that they secure the person of a citizen from assaults, they would likewise provide for the security of his reputation.[14]

With ratification of the federal Constitution, Franklin retired from public service but not from life. With help from grandson Benjamin Bache, he was able to keep up a lively correspondence with old friends such as Jean Baptiste Le Roy, to whom he addressed his most celebrated remark. Daniel Defoe's *Political History of the Devil* (1726) had insisted that people more readily believe the devil has a cloven hoof than "things as certain as death and taxes."[15] Franklin, as Poor Richard once did with well-worn proverbs, distilled Defoe's remark to its essence.

Our new Constitution is now established, and has an appearance that promises permanency; but in this world nothing can be said to be certain, except death and taxes.[16]

Franklin's familiar letters held other examples of recycling early material. In January 1722 the *New-England Courant* had printed the quip about a Connecticut trader who had cornered the market in onions but could not sell them: "The more they are cursed, the more they grow."[17] In May 1785 Franklin nourished that allusion into a full-blown apologue on Londoners who claimed America was going broke.

Franklin would often acknowledge his sources. Sometimes,

too, he fabricated his own sources, as with the revenge play about Rodrigo and the reluctant Apothecary or the fable of the two-headed snake who could not make up its mind. More often his material lay embedded in an extraordinary memory, as when he exchanged symptoms with septuagenarian George Whatley. In jesting about the cost of living so long, Franklin paraphrased verses from Walter Pope's, "The Old Man's Wish"—"May I govern my Passions with an absolute sway, Grow wiser and better as my Strength wears away, Without Gout or Stone, by a gentle Decay"—and segued into an old joke.

> But what signifies our Wishing? Things happen, after all, as they will happen. I have sung that *wishing Song* a thousand times, when I was young, and now find, at Fourscore, that the three Contraries have befallen me, being subject to the Gout and the Stone, and not being yet Master of all my Passions. Like the proud Girl in my Country, who wished and resolv'd not to marry a Parson, nor a Presbyterian, nor an Irishman; and at length found herself married to an Irish Presbyterian Parson.[18]

This is not to suggest that octogenarian Franklin had lost his creative juices, either verbal or visual. Only half in jest, he explained why the population of abandoned children in Paris exploded in thirty years from every tenth child to every third child, and fifteen years later "may now amount to one half," which he blamed on mothers refusing to breast-feed their babes.

> Is it right to encourage this monstrous Deficiency of natural Affection? A Surgeon I met with here excused the Women of Paris, by saying, seriously, that they *could not* give suck, "Car," dit il, "elles n'ont de tetons" [Because, said he, they have no teats]. He assur'd me it was a Fact, and bade me look at them, and observe how flat they were on the Breast; "they have nothing more there," said he, "than I have upon the Back of my hand." I have since thought that there might be some Truth in his Observation, and

that, possibly, Nature, finding they made no use of Bubbies, has left off giving them any.[19]

Particularly in writing to family, Franklin's memory would overflow with both verbal and visual humor. In recollecting how he nearly electrocuted himself in an experiment, he cursed his own stupidity: "a Match for that of the Irishman, Sister told me of, who to divert his Wife pour'd the Bottle of Gun Powder on the live Coal; or of that Other, about to steal Powder, made a Hole in the Cask with a Hott Iron."[20] Trying to laugh at being disabled, he visualized himself as carried by a balloon, "being led by a string held by a man walking on the ground."[21] In reassuring his sister Jane Mecom about her spelling, Franklin recollected a phonetic system he had devised twenty years earlier.[22]

You need not be concern'd in writing to me about your bad Spelling: for in my Opinion as our Alphabet now stands, the bad Spelling, or what is call'd so, is generally the best, as conforming to the Sound of the Letters and of the Words. To give you an Instance, A Gentleman receiving a Letter in which were these Words, Not finding Brown at hom, I delivered your Meseg to his yf. The Gentleman finding it bad Spelling, and therefore not very intelligible, call'd his Lady to help him read it. Between them they pick'd out the meaning of all but the y f, which they could not understand. The Lady propos'd calling her Chambermaid; for Betty, says she, has the best Knack at reading bad Spelling of any one I know. Betty came, and was surpriz'd that neither Sir nor Madam could tell what y, f was; why, says she, y, f spells Wife, what else can it spell? And indeed it is a much better as well as shorter method of Spelling Wife, than by Doubleyou, i f, e, which in reality spells Double-yifey.[23]

Jane Mecom reported a typical unintended consequence of his fame as humorist. She told Franklin that Boston newspapers honored him, "but some chuse to Embelish the Language to there own fancy the Storey of the French man with the Pocker was a good story when you tould it but it apears to me there was none of your D—n . . . you Souls in it."[24] The Philadelphia magazine, *American Museum,* had also just printed a profane version of the poker story. Franklin reassured his sister Jane with a story symbolizing his lifelong practice.

There was no swearing in the story of the poker, when I told it. The late new dresser of it was, probably, the same, or perhaps akin to him, who, in relating a dispute that happened between Queen Anne and the Archbishop of Canterbury, concerning a vacant mitre, which the Queen was for bestowing on a person the Archbishop thought unworthy, made both the Queen and the Archbishop swear three or four thumping oaths in every sentence of the discussion, and the Archbishop at last gained his point. One present at this tale, being surprised, said, "But did the Queen and the Archbishop swear so at one another?" "O no, no," says the relator; "that is only *my way* of telling the story."[25]

On his deathbed, Franklin continued to compose the story of his life and revise what he had written previously. Over the years since 1771 he had shaped the first part at least as a comic epic in prose with himself as picaresque hero on the model of Fielding's *Tom Jones,* prevailing over the wickedness of others and especially over his own animal spirits.[26] On a narrative framework, he now strung apologues about critical events in his past. One episode dramatized the autobiography's controlling idea in telling how, becalmed off Block Island, vegetarian principles prevented him from eating cod: "None of them had or ever could do us any Injury *that might justify the Slaughter"*—

All this was very reasonable. But I had formerly been a great Lover of Fish, & when this came out of the Frying Pan, it smelt admirably well. I balanc'd some time between Principle & Inclination: At length I recollected, that when Fish were opened, I saw smaller Fish taken out of their Stomachs: Then, thought I, if you eat one another, I don't see why we may n't eat you. So I din'd upon Cod very heartily. . . . So convenient a thing it is to be a *reasonable Creature,* since it enables one to find or make a Reason for every thing one has a mind to do.[27]

Apologues embedded amusing lessons in living reasonably. Worn down by a self-devised system of behavior modification, Franklin confessed, "I was almost ready to give up the Attempt and content my self with a faulty Character," deceiving himself that "a perfect Character might be attended with the Inconvenience of being envied and hated; and that a benevolent Man should allow a few Faults in himself, to keep his Friends in Countenance"—

Like the Man who in buying an Ax of a Smith my neighbour, desired to have the broad whole of its Surface as bright as the Edge; the Smith consented to grind it bright for him if he would turn the Wheel. He turn'd while the Smith to fatigue him press'd the broad Face of the Ax hard & heavily on the Stone, which made the Turning very fatiguing. The Man came every now & then from the Wheel to see how the Work went on, and at length would take his Ax as it was without farther Grinding. No, says the Smith, Turn on, turn on; we shall have it bright by and by; as yet 'tis only speckled. Yes, says the Man; but—*I think I like a speckled Ax best.*[28]

Franklin sometimes reversed the formula, so that the commentary following the apologue reinforced the irony, as in the episode of an Indian orator apologizing for his people's behavior during a long night of drunken noise.

The Orator acknowledg'd the Fault, but laid it upon the Rum; and then endeavour'd to excuse the Rum, by saying, "The great Spirit who made all things made every thing for some Use, and whatever Use he design'd them for, that Use they should always be put to; Now, when he made Rum, he said, *'Let this be for Indians to get drunk with.'* And so it must be so."—And indeed if it be the Design of Providence to extirpate these Savages in order to make room for Cultivators of the Earth, it seems not impossible that

Rum may be the appointed Means. It has already annihilated all the Tribes who formerly inhabited the Seacoast."[29]

> Franklin used comic scenes most artfully in shaping our attitude toward the leading characters in his life with or without authorial comment. The best example would be the way he caricatured his early boss, Samuel Keimer. In life, Keimer had once been Daniel Defoe's printer. He had been jailed in London in the cause of a free press. Franklin, saying nothing of this, showed him to be a ridiculous eccentric hell-bent for bankruptcy. In fact, from Philadelphia, Keimer emigrated to Barbados, where his *Barbadoes Gazette* became the first newspaper in North America to appear twice weekly for several years, a success that eluded Franklin's *Pennsylvania Gazette*, after only a few months.

He retain'd a good deal of his old Enthusiasms, and lov'd a Dispute. We therefore had many. I work'd him so with my Socratic Method and had trapann'd him so often by Questions apparently so distant from any Point we had in hand, and yet by degrees led to the Point, that at last he grew ridiculously cautious, and would hardly answer me the most common Question, without asking first, "What do you intend to infer from that?" However it gave him so high an Opinion of my Abilities in the Confuting Way, that he seriously propos'd my being his Colleague in a Project he had of setting up a new Sect. He was to preach the Doctrines, and I was to confound all Opponents. When he came to explain with me upon the Doctrines, I found several Conundrums which I objected to, unless I might have my Way a little too, and introduced some of mine. Keimer wore his Beard at full Length, because somewhere in the Mosaic Law it is said, "thou shalt not mar the Corners of thy Beard." He likewise kept the seventh day Sabbath; and these two Points were Essentials with him. I dislik'd both, but agreed to admit them upon Condition of his adopting the Doctrine of using no animal Food. I doubt, says he, my Constitution will not bear that. I assur'd him it would, & that he would be the better for it. He was usually a great Gourmandizer, and I promis'd myself some Diversion in half-starving him. Hearing me talk of that Mode of Living, he said he would try it if I would keep him Company. I did so for three Months.

We had our Vegetables dress'd and brought to us regularly by a Woman in the Neighbourhood, who had from me a list of 40 Dishes to be prepar'd for us at different times, in which there was neither Fish Flesh nor Fowl, and the Whim suited me the better at this time from the Cheapness of it, not costing above 18 pence Sterling each, per Week. . . . I went on pleasantly, but poor Keimer tir'd of the Project, long'd for the Flesh Pots of Egypt, and order'd a roast Pig, invited me & two Women Friends to dine with him, but it being brought too soon upon the Table, he could not resist the Temptation and ate it all up before we came. [30]

In his sixty-eight years as a professional writer, Franklin endured a cycle of bad luck with his petitions to the government. In the 1750s, his petition to curb Pennsylvania's proprietors, initially troubled because Franklin did not follow standard procedure, dragged through British courts for years. In the 1770s, as an agent for Massachusetts, his petition to curb Governor Hutchinson gave his enemies occasion to humiliate Franklin publicly with insults and allegations of treason. In the 1780s, Congress repeatedly denied Franklin's personal petitions to be allowed to return from France, and once he had returned, even refused to compensate him for expenses incurred while there. In his last days as president of the Pennsylvania Abolition Society, Franklin petitioned Congress to curb the slave trade.

The *Federal Gazette* (25 March 1790) printed a letter as from Historicus reacting to a speech by James Jackson of Georgia in Congress. Jackson had urged Congress to reject Franklin's petition. Jackson, quoting freely from John Millar's *Origin of Distinction of Ranks* (1771), argued that slaves were better off here than in Africa, that slavery had scriptural authority, and that planters like himself would suffer economically. Historicus offers the same points from a speech made by a fictional Sidi Mehemet Ibrahim a hundred years earlier respecting Christian slavery in Algeria, where in the 1790s it still flourished. Except for exaggerating the number of Christian slaves in Sidi Mehemet's supposed era (cited as 50,000 versus the actual 18,000), Franklin used a simple analogy, substituting "Christian slaves" for African slaves.[31]

Historicus concludes the fictional address and adds the Prescient comment:

> "How grossly are they mistaken in imagining Slavery to be disallow'd by the Alcoran! Are not the two Precepts, to quote no more, "*Masters, treat your Slaves with kindness; Slaves, serve your Masters with Cheerfulness and Fidelity*," clear Proofs to the contrary? Nor can the Plundering of Infidels be in that sacred Book forbidden, since it is well known from it, that God has given the World, and all that it contains, to his faithful Mussulmen, who are to enjoy it out of Right as fast as they can concquer it. Let us then hear no more of this detestable Proposition, the Manumission of Christian Slaves, the Adoption of which would, by depreciating our Lands and Houses, and thereby depriving so many good Citizens of their Properties, create universal Discontent, and provoke Insurrections, to the endangering of Government and producing general Confusion. I have therefore no doubt, but this wise Council will prefer the Comfort and Happiness of a whole Nation of true Believers to the Whim of a few *Erika*, and dismiss their Petition."
>
> The result was, as Martin tells us, that the Divan came to this Resolution; "The Doctrine, that Plundering and Enslaving the Christians is unjust, is at best *problematical*; but that it is the Interest of this State to continue the Practice, is clear; therefore let the Petition be rejected."
>
> And it was rejected accordingly.
>
> And since like Motives are apt to produce in the minds of Men like Opinions and Resolutions, may we not . . . venture to predict, from this account, that the Petitions to the Parliament of England for abolishing the Slave-Trade, to say nothing of other Legistatures, and the Debates upon them, will

have a similar Conclusion? I am, Sir, your constant Reader and humble Servant,

Historicus

From experience, Franklin must have anticipated the result, if not the acrimony, of the debate in Congress. His friend Elias Boudinot of New Jersey rose to defend him against insult ("The firmness of his mind has been suspected") and ignorance ("An ingenious parable of his has been read to the committee, but its application is totally mistaken"). His once-celebrated irony bombinated in the void as his final petition lay rejected.[32]

Franklin's identifying the United States Congress with despotic Algeria reflected his anger at Congress's neglecting his petition to be compensated for services in France. He had warned of the nation's vulnerability to despots at the end of the Constitutional Convention when Elizabeth Powel, wife of Philadelphia's mayor, asked, "Well, Doctor, what have we got—a republic or a monarchy," and he replied, "A republic if you can keep it."[33] He was not laughing.

Notes

Introduction

1. Bliven 12.
2. Franklin, *Papers* 7:246.
3. Abigail Adams 1:64.
4. Priestley 25:393.
5. Zall, ed., *Wit and Wisdom* 58.
6. Ibid., 43.
7. Ibid., 48.
8. Mazzei 215.
9. Balzac 2:115.
10. Zall, "Portrait" 53–65.
11. Zall, ed., *Franklin on Franklin* 80.
12. Ibid., 62.
13. Ibid., 165.
14. Ibid., 190.
15. Franklin, *Papers* 13:142.
16. Zall, ed., *Franklin on Franklin* 116.
17. Ibid., 243.
18. Ibid., 246.
19. Ibid., 254.
20. Franklin, *Autobiography* 172.
21. Franklin, *Papers* 22:85.
22. Ibid., 26:223.
23. *Documentary History of Ratification*, 13:214.
24. John Adams 1:663–64.
25. Zall, ed., *Franklin on Franklin* 279.
26. Franklin, *Writings*, ed. Smyth, 9:687.
27. Zall, ed., *Franklin on Franklin* 276.
28. *Pennsylvania Gazette*, 2 August 1738.
29. Zall, ed., *Ben Franklin Laughing*, 87.
30. Zall, ed., *Jefferson on Jefferson* 61.
31. Zall, ed., *Ben Franklin Laughing*, 140.
32. Zall, ed., *Abe Lincoln Laughing* 42.
33. Zall, ed., *Franklin on Franklin* 286.

Chapter 1

1. Jorgenson, "Sidelights" 217.
2. Lemay, "Benjamin Franklin" 205–6.
3. Tourtellot 337.
4. Excerpts are from the *New-England Courant,* 2 April–8 October 1722, which are reprinted in Franklin, *Papers* 1:8–45.
5. Zall, ed., *Wit and Wisdom* 47.
6. Defoe, *Moll Flanders* 58.
7. Addison and Steele 2:122n.
8. Lemay, *Calendar* 5.
9. Preface to "Horae Lyricae, 1706" in Watts 100.
10. *Guardian* (10 June 1713) 288–90.
11. Tourtellot 382.
12. Zall, ed., *Wit and Wisdom* 20–24; Mencken 266.
13. Franklin, *Writings,* ed. Lemay, 1326.
14. Lemay, "Benjamin Franklin" 205, 210.

Chapter 2

1. Kobre 54.
2. Cook 62–70.
3. The Busy-Body series in Franklin, *Writings,* ed. Lemay, 95.
4. *Pennsylvania Gazette,* 13 March 1729.
5. March 4, 1729; Franklin, *Writings,* ed. Lemay, 110.
6. Addison and Steele 2:110.
7. Butterfield 3:33.
8. Facsimile of Yale University Library copy, in Franklin, *Papers* 1:111.
9. Addison and Steele 4:580.
10. Franklin, *Writings,* ed. Lemay, 1370.
11. Swift, *Tale* 173.
12. Ibid., 171.

Chapter 3

1. Besides *Poor Richard,* the almanacs discussed are in the Huntington Library: *American Almanac,* accession number 12615; *Poor Robin* (London), 336368; *Poor Robin* (Newport, R.I.), 152419; Saunder's *Apollo Anglicanus,* 336368.
2. Miller 26.
3. Franklin, *Complete Poor Richard Almanacks* 1:ix.
4. Franklin, *Writings,* ed. Lemay, 1397.
5. Howell, *Lexicon Tetraglotton* (1660), originally entitled *Paroimiographia* (1659).

6. Samples in parentheses are from Howell's *Tetraglotton* (1560) with no regular pagination.
7. Swift, *Predictions for the Year 1712*, 5.
8. *American Almanack* (1734).
9. *American Almanack* (1735).
10. Sappenfield 134–35.
11. Blackwell 4–5.
12. Zall, ed., *Franklin on Franklin* 138.
13. Pencak 183.
14. "To the Reader," *American Almanack* (1743), in Shipton and Mooney, eds.
15. Wolf 2780.

Chapter 4

1. Franklin, *Papers* 4:199.
2. Thomas Penn to Richard Peters, June 1740, in Illick 194–95.
3. Franklin, *Writings,* ed. Lemay, 298.
4. Franklin, *Papers* 3:30–31.
5. Franklin, *Writings,* ed. Lemay, 302–3.
6. Hall 94–96.
7. Ibid., 100–101.
8. "The Speech of Miss Polly Baker," in Lemay, ed., *Oldest Revolutionary* 107.
9. Franklin, *Papers* 7:341n.

Chapter 5

1. Howell, *Epistolae Ho-Elianae* 1–2.
2. Franklin, *Papers* 8:152–53.
3. Selden 100–101.
4. Franklin, *Papers* 9:212–13.
5. Ibid., 9:259–60.
6. Potts 56–57.
7. Franklin, *Papers* 10:83.
8. Herodotus 217; Crane 33n–34n.
9. Jorgenson, "Benjamin Franklin and Rabelais" 538–40; Lemay, "Franklin in France" 127.
10. *Public Advertiser* (London), 22 May 1765; Crane 33–34.
11. Crane xvi.
12. Lopez, *Mon Cher Papa* 19.
13. Galton 54.
14. (London) *Gazetteer,* 14 January 1766.

15. Thomas 250.
16. *Pennsylvania Chronicle,* 23 March 1767; Franklin, *Papers* 13:184.
17. Franklin, *Papers* 13:24–42; Franklin, *Writings,* ed. Lemay, 580.
18. *Public Advertiser,* 23 January 1766; Crane 56–57.
19. Franklin, *Papers* 14:255.
20. Franklin, *Celebrated Mrs. Pilkington's Jests* 80–84.
21. Franklin, *Papers* 17:220–26.
22. Ibid., 17:239.
23. *Public Advertiser,* 2 January 1770; Crane 166–67.
24. Franklin, *Papers* 18:200–202.
25. Ibid., 19:301–2.
26. Zall, ed., *Franklin on Franklin* 255.

Chapter 6

1. Franklin, *Papers* 20:457–58.
2. Bacon 6:444.
3. Franklin, *Papers* 20:391–99; Franklin, *Writings,* ed. Lemay, 689–97.
4. Franklin, *Papers* 20:412.
5. Simson 152–57.
6. *Annual Register of World Events . . . 1772,* 31–34.
7. (London) *Public Advertiser,* 22 September 1773; Franklin, *Papers* 20:414–18.
8. Franklin, *Papers* 20:458.
9. Zall, ed., *Franklin on Franklin* 249.
10. Ibid., 248–49.
11. Crane 238; Franklin, *Papers* 20:455.
12. Franklin, *Papers* 20:464.
13. Donoughue 34.
14. *Public Advertiser,* 16 February 1774; Franklin, *Papers* 21:101.
15. Crane 263n; Franklin, *Papers* 21:220n.
16. Crane 262–64; Franklin, *Papers* 21:221–22.
17. Franklin, *Papers* 21:72–73.
18. Priestley 25:393.
19. Zall, ed., *Franklin on Franklin* 51–52.
20. Ibid., 50–51.

Chapter 7

1. Zall, ed., *Franklin on Franklin* 281.
2. Franklin, *Papers* 23:549–50.
3. Ibid., 23:298–99.
4. Lemay, "Franklin in France" 137

5. Franklin, *Papers* 29:613.
6. Lopez, *Mon Cher Papa* 18–19.
7. Franklin, *Papers* 30:514.
8. Franklin, *Writings,* ed. Lemay, 965.
9. Zall, ed., *Ben Franklin Laughing* 105–6.
10. Lopez, *Mon Cher Papa* 58.
11. Franklin, *Writings,* ed. Lemay, 925.
12. Lopez, *Mon Cher Papa* 89.
13. Translated from facsimile in Livingston 42–43.
14. Ibid., 34–35.
15. Franklin, *Complete Works* 6:275–77.
16. Lowell 18–19.
17. Ibid., 25.
18. Franklin, *Complete Works* 6:77n.
19. Franklin, *Papers* 24:9.
20. Franklin, *Complete Works* 6:74–78 (capitals added).
21. Mitchell 273–74.
22. Henry 3:220.
23. Franklin, *Writings,* ed. Smyth, 8:562.
24. Ibid., 8:433.
25. Fenton 435.
26. Facsimile in Livingston 58–59.

Chapter 8

1. Zall, ed., *Franklin on Franklin* 265.
2. Pepper 92n.
3. Zall, ed., *Wit and Wisdom* 119–20.
4. Wolfe 49.
5. Reprinted in *American Museum* 7 (June 1790): 317–19.
6. Gillispie 34–35.
7. Hale and Hale 2:284–85.
8. Franklin, *Papers* 32:396–97; Lopez, "Background," Franklin, *Bagatelles from Passy* 77–78.
9. Livingston 42.
10. Franklin, *Papers* 32:398–400.
11. Franklin, *Writings,* ed. Smyth, 9:163–65.
12. Ibid., 9:168.
13. Ibid., 9:177.
14. Amacher 80, 156.
15. Aldrich 402.
16. Zall, ed., *Ben Franklin Laughing* 49.

17. Franklin, *Papers* 37:445.
18. Zall, ed., *Ben Franklin Laughing* 51–52.

Chapter 9

1. *Pennsylvania Gazette,* 9 September, 5 October, 2 November 1785.
2. Zall, ed., *Wit and Wisdom* 11.
3. Van Doren, *Benjamin Franklin* 735–36.
4. "Madison's Notes, 5 June 1787," in Benton, ed., 2:1315.
5. Zall, ed., *Ben Franklin Laughing* 93–94.
6. *Worcester Magazine* 4 (October 1787): 112.
7. Zall, *Washington on Washington* 92.
8. Franklin, *Writings,* ed. Smyth, 10:57–58.
9. Vinson 192.
10. Franklin, *Writings,* ed. Lemay, 1149–50.
11. *Independent Gazeteer,* 24 November 1788.
12. Centinel I, *Independent Gazeteer,* 5 October 1787.
13. Schwartz 2:1148.
14. *Federal Gazette,* 12 September 1789.
15. Defoe, *Works* 10:246.
16. Franklin, *Writings,* ed. Smyth, 10:69.
17. Zall, ed., *Ben Franklin Laughing* 52.
18. Franklin, *Writings,* ed. Smyth, 9:333.
19. Ibid., 334.
20. Zall, ed., *Franklin on Franklin* 172.
21. Ibid., 285.
22. Franklin, *Writings,* ed. Lemay, 626–32.
23. Van Doren, ed., *Letters* 273–74.
24. Ibid., 317.
25. Ibid., 319.
26. Zall, *Franklin's Autobiography* 32–40.
27. Zall, *Franklin on Franklin* 50–51.
28. Ibid., 115–16.
29. Ibid., 164–65.
30. Ibid., 51–52.
31. *Federal Gazette,* 25 March 1790.
32. [Benton], *Abridgment* 1:238.
33. McHenry 618.

Sources

Adams, Abigail, Jr. *Journal and Correspondence of Miss Adams.* Edited by Carolyn A. DeWindt. 2 vols. New York: Wiley and Putnam, 1841.

Adams, John. *Works.* Edited by Charles Francis Adams. 10 vols. Boston: Little, Brown, 1856.

Addison, Joseph, and Richard Steele. *The Spectator.* Edited by Donald F. Bond. 5 vols. Oxford: Clarendon, 1965.

Aldrich, Alfred Owen. "Franklin's Deistical Indians." *Proceedings of the American Philosophical Society* 94 (1950): 398–410.

Amacher, Richard E. *Franklin's Wit and Folly: The Bagatelles.* New Brunswick, N.J.: Rutgers University Press, 1953.

American Almanack. Edited by Titan Leeds. Philadelphia: Bradford, 1734–1735, 1743.

Annual Register of World Events . . . 1772. London: J. Dodsley, 1773.

Bacon, Francis. *Works.* Edited by James Spedding, Robert Ellis, and Douglas Heath. 14 vols. London: Longmans, 1857–1874.

Balzac, Honoré. *Ilusión Perdues.* 2 vols. Paris: Levy, 1879.

[Benton, Thomas Hart]. *Benton's Abridgment of the Debates in Congress,* 16 vols. New York: Appleton, 1857–61.

Benton, Welbourn E., ed. *1787: Drafting the Constitution.* College Station: Texas A&M University Press, 1986.

Blackwell, Henry. *Happenings of Future Years Foretold in Old Welsh Almanacs.* New York: Privately printed, 1910.

Bliven, Bruce. "Benjamin Franklin." *Reader's Digest,* May 1976, 11–12.

Butterfield, Lyman H. "B. Franklin's Epitaph." *New Colophon,* n.s. 3 (1950): 9–30.

The Celebrated Mrs. Pilkington's Jests. 2d ed. London: W. Nicoll, 1764.

Cook, Elizabeth C. *Literary Influences in Colonial Newspapers, 1704–50.* New York: Columbia, 1912.

Crane, Verner C. *Benjamin Franklin's Letters to the Press.* Chapel Hill: University of North Carolina Press, 1950.

Defoe, Daniel. *Fortunes and Misfortunes of the Famous Moll Flanders.* Edited by G[eorge] A. Starr. London: Oxford University Press, 1971.

———. *Works.* Edited by Walter Scott. 20 vols. London: Oxford University Press, 1840.

Documentary History of the Ratification of the Constitution. Ed. Merrill Jensen, et al. 18 vols. Madison: State Historical Society of Wisconsin, 1976–95.

Donoughue, Bernard. *British Politics and the American Revolution.* London: Macmillan, 1964.

Fenton, William N. *The Great Law and the Longhouse.* Norman: University of Oklahoma Press, 1998.

Franklin, Benjamin. *Autobiography.* Edited by J. A. Leo Lemay and P. M. Zall. New York: Norton, 1986.

———. *Bagatelles from Passy.* New York: Eakins Press, 1967.

———. *Complete Poor Richard Almanacks.* Edited by Whitfield J. Bell Jr. 2 vols. Barre, Mass.: Imprint Society, 1970.

———. *Complete Works.* Edited by John Bigelow. 12 vols. New York: Putnam, 1868–1904.

———. *Papers of Benjamin Franklin.* Edited by Ellen R. Cohn et al. New Haven, Conn.: Yale University Press, 1959–.

———. *Writings.* Edited by J. A. Leo Lemay. New York: Library of America, 1987.

———. *Writings of Benjamin Franklin.* Edited by Albert H. Smyth. 10 vols. New York: Macmillan, 1905–1907.

Galton, F. W., ed. *Select Documents . . . The Tailoring Trade.* London: Longmans, Green, 1896.

Gillispie, Charles Coulston. *The Montgolfier Brothers and the Invention of Aviation, 1783–84.* Princeton, N.J.: Princeton University Press, 1983.

Guardian, The. Edited by John C. Stephens. Lexington: University Press of Kentucky, 1982.

Hale, Edward E., and E. E. Hale Jr. *Franklin in France.* 2 vols. Boston: Roberts, 1888.

Hall, Max. *Benjamin Franklin and Polly Baker.* Chapel Hill: University of North Carolina Press, 1960.

Henry, William Wirt, ed. *Patrick Henry.* 3 vols. New York: Scribner, 1891.

Herodotus. *History.* Translated by Henry Cary. London: Bell and Daldy, 1872.

Howell, James. *Epistolae Ho-Elianae: Familiar Letters Domestic and Forren.* 2d ed. London: Humphrey Moseley, 1650.

———. *Lexicon Tetraglotton.* London: S. Thomson, 1660.

Illick, Joseph E. *Colonial Pennsylvania.* New York: Scribners, 1976.

Jorgenson, Chester E. "Benjamin Franklin and Rabelais." *Classical Journal* 29 (1934): 538–40.

———. "Sidelights on Benjamin Franklin's Principles of Rhetoric." *Revue Anglo-Américaine* 11 (1933–1934): 208–22.

Kobre, Sidney. *Development of the Colonial Newspaper.* Pittsburgh: Colonial Press, 1944.

Lemay, J. A. Leo. "Benjamin Franklin." In *Major Writers of Early American Literature.* Edited by Everett Emerson. Madison: University of Wisconsin Press, 1972.

———. *Calendar of American Poetry . . . Through 1765.* Worcester: American Antiquarian Society, 1972.

———. "Franklin and France." In *Benjamin Franklin: Des Lumières a Nos Jours,* edited by Gerard Hugues and Daniel Royot. Lyon: Didier, 1991.

———, ed. *The Oldest Revolutionary.* Philadelphia: University of Pennsylvania Press, 1976.

Livingston, Luther S. *Franklin and His Press at Passy.* New York: Grolier, 1914.

Lopez, Claude-Anne. "Background." In *Bagatelles from Passy.* New York: Eakins Press, 1967.

———. *Mon Cher Papa: Franklin and the Ladies of Paris.* New Haven, Conn.: Yale University Press, 1966.

Lowell, Edward J. *Hessians and Other German Auxiliaries of Great Britain in the Revolution.* New York: Harper, 1884.

Mazzei, Philip. *Researches in the United States.* Translated by Constance D. Sherman. Charlottesville: University Press of Virginia, 1976.

McHenry, James. "Papers." *American Historical Review* 11 (1906): 595–624.

Mencken, Henry Louis. *The American Language: Supplement One.* New York: Knopf, 1945.

Miller, William C. *Franklin's Philadelphia Printing.* Philadelphia: American Philosophical Society, 1974.

Mitchell, Broadus. *Price of Independence.* New York: Oxford University Press, 1974.

Pencak, William. "Politics and Ideology in Poor Richard's Almanac." *Pennsylvania Magazine of History and Biography* 116 (1992): 183–211.

Pepper, William. *Medical Side of Benjamin Franklin, The.* Philadelphia: Campbell, 1911.

Potts, William. *Banbury Cross and Rhyme.* Banbury: Guardian Office, 1930.

Priestley, Joseph. *Theological and Miscellaneous Works.* 25 vols. Edited by J. T. Rutt. Hackney: Smallfield, 1831.

Sappenfield, James A. *A Sweet Instruction.* Carbondale: Southern Illinois University Press, 1973.

Schwartz, Bernard. *The Bill of Rights: A Documentary History.* 2 vols. New York: McGraw-Hill, 1971.

Selden, John. *Table-Talk.* Edited by Edward Arber. London: Murray, 1868.

Shipton, Clifford K., and James E. Mooney, eds. *Early American Imprints to 1800.* Worcester: American Antiquarian Society, 1969.

Simson, George. "Legal Sources for Franklin's 'Edict.'" *American Literature* 32 (1960): 152–57.

Swift, Jonathan. *A Tale of a Tub.* 2d ed. Edited by Adolph C. Guthkelch and D. Nichol Smith. Oxford: Clarendon, 1958.

———. *Predictions for the Year 1712 . . . by Isaac Bickerstaff.* 1712.

Thomas, P. D. G. *British Politics and the Stamp Act Crisis.* Oxford: Clarendon, 1975.

Tourtellot, Arthur B. *Benjamin Franklin: The Shaping of Genius.* Garden City, N.Y.: Doubleday, 1977.

Van Doren, Carl. *Benjamin Franklin.* New York: Viking, 1938.

———, ed. *Letters of Benjamin Franklin and Jane Mecom.* Princeton, N.J.: Princeton University Press, 1950.

Vinson, Michael. "The Society for Political Inquiries: Limits of Republican Discourse." *Pennsylvania Magazine of History and Biography* 113 (April 1989): 185–205.

Watts, Isaac. *Divine Songs.* Edited by J. H. P. Pafford. London: Oxford University Press, 1971.

Wolf, Edwin 2d. "Benjamin Franklin's Way to Wealth." *AB Bookman's Weekly* 58 (17 May 1976): 2780–89.

Wolfe, John J. *Brandy, Balloons and Lamps; Ami Argand, 1750–1803.* Carbondale: Southern Illinois University Press, 1999.

Zall, Paul M. "Portrait of the Autobiographer as an Old Artificer." In *The Oldest Revolutionary,* edited by J. A. Leo Lemay. Philadelphia: University of Pennsylvania Press, 1976.

Zall, Paul M., ed. *Abe Lincoln Laughing.* Berkeley: University of California Press, 1982.

———. *Ben Franklin Laughing.* Berkeley: University of California Press, 1980.

———. *Franklin's Autobiography: A Model Life.* Boston: C. K. Hall, 1989.

———. *Franklin on Franklin.* Lexington: University Press of Kentucky, 2000.

———. *Jefferson on Jefferson.* Lexington: University Press of Kentucky, 2002.

———. *Washington on Washington.* Lexington: University Press of Kentucky, 2003.

———. *Wit and Wisdom of the Founding Fathers.* Hopewell: ECCO, 1996.

Index

Index

Index